From the Path to Leadership Series

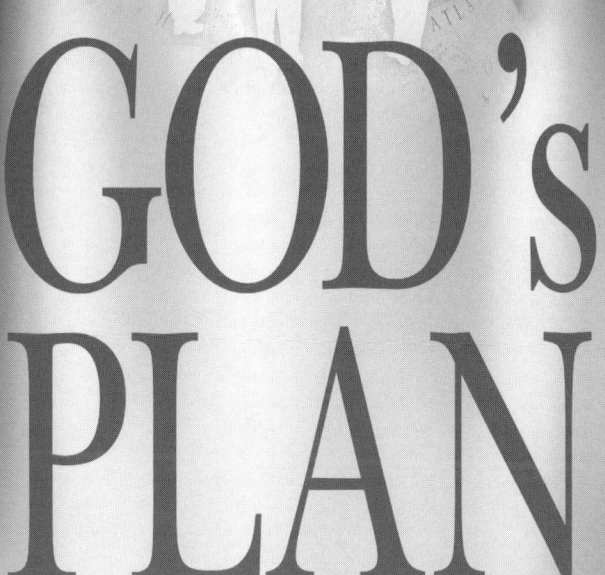

GOD'S PLAN
for the CHURCH

From the Path to Leadership Series

GOD'S PLAN
for the CHURCH

Andre Butler

God's Plan for the Church

Copyright 2006 by Faith Christian Center

Editorial Notes: All references to the names and attributes of God are capitalized. We have chosen not to capitalize the name "satan" and related names, even at the cost of violating grammatical rules.

All rights reserved. Contents and/or cover may not be reproduced in whole or in part in any form without the express written consent of the Publisher.

Unless otherwise indicated, all Scripture quotations in this book are from the King James Version of the *Holy Bible*.

The Amplified® Bible, Copyright © 1954, 1958, 1962, 1964, 1965, 1987 by The Lockman Foundation. Used by permission.

Young's Literal Translation of the Holy Bible. Public domain.

ISBN-10: 0-9768299-2-4
ISBN-13: 978-0-9768299-2-8

Published by Faith Christian Center
3059 S. Cobb Drive
Smyrna, GA 30080
www.fccga.com

Printed in the USA

Interior book design by Faith Instructional Design, Inc.
www.faithid.biz

Table of Contents

Introduction 1

Chapter 1 3
God's Strategy for Building the Church

Chapter 2 29
Benefits of Small Group Involvement

Chapter 3 47
The Call to Disciple Others

Chapter 4 67
Be Like Jesus and Get Your Twelve

Appendix 85
Touch Group Testimonies

Notes 105

Introduction

God has big plans for His church. In fact, He desires that His church grow to such a place in the Earth that satan's kingdom will not be able to prevail against it. One day, the whole Earth will be filled and ruled by the kingdom of God, and believers will reign with Jesus.

In order for God to build His church, however, He has to build His people, because the church is not a building; the church is the people of God. The early church met not only in the temple but also from house to house. If we want to have the same results they had—revival and exponential growth—we must follow God's blueprint for church growth.

One of the key markers in God's blueprint is the establishment of small groups of people who meet in private homes and open themselves to receiving all the benefits of blessings and growth. These groups are called by different names. Some churches call them cell groups, because cells make up a body, and the people of God are called the body of Christ. In the church I pastor, these groups are called Touch Groups, because we want to emphasize the relational nature of fulfilling God's commandment to love Him and one another.

Every believer has a role to play in growing the church of God. This book explores God's plan to win souls, consolidate[1] new Christians into the body of Christ, and disciple them until they are able to go forth and make disciples also. I challenge you to listen and respond to His call.

Chapter 1

God's Strategy for Building the Church

In the following Scripture passage revealing the foundation of the church, Jesus asked His disciples a question:

Matthew 16
[13]When Jesus came into the coasts of Caesarea Philippi, he asked his disciples, saying, Whom do men say that I the Son of man am?
[14]And they said, Some say that thou art John the Baptist: some, Elias; and others, Jeremias, or one of the prophets.
[15]He saith unto them, But whom say ye that I am?
[16]And Simon Peter answered and said, Thou art the Christ, the Son of the living God.
[17]And Jesus answered and said unto him, Blessed art thou, Simon Barjona: for flesh and blood hath not revealed it unto thee, but my Father which is in heaven.

In other words, Jesus said, "Simon, no one told you this; you did not figure it out on your own. You received this knowledge from the Spirit of God." That is how revelation comes—from the Holy Spirit to your spirit. But notice the next thing Jesus said:

> Matthew 16:18
> And I say also unto thee, That thou art Peter, and upon this rock I will build my church; and the gates of hell shall not prevail against it.

The Greek word for "Peter" is *petros,* which means "small rock." The Greek word for "rock" is *petra,* which means "large rock," such as the Rock of Gibraltar.

The Catholic church has interpreted this Scripture to mean that the church was going to be built upon Peter, but Jesus was saying the church was going to be built upon revelation. Jesus said, *"Upon this rock"*—upon revelation—*"I will build my church."* The "large rock" is revelation, and this is the only trustworthy foundation for the church.

Notice Jesus said, *"I will build my church,"* and He also says, *"I **will**."* He was prophesying that the church would be established as a result of Him. Not only would it be established, but it would also be built up—it would continue to increase in size.

The Greek word for "build" means "to construct." God's will is to build His church, and God's church is His people, not a building. In fact, the word *church* means "called-out ones" or "the assembly." But whether you are talking about a church building or the body of Christ, both take time to construct. Neither is built overnight.

To construct a building, you have to prepare the ground before you lay the foundation. That is what God did with His church—His called-out ones. He spent four thousand years preparing the ground before He laid the foundation called Jesus. It has taken time—and it will continue to take time—to fully complete the task of building the church.

God's Building Materials

What does God use to build His church?

> 1 Peter 2:5
> Ye also, as lively stones, are built up a spiritual house, an holy priesthood, to offer up spiritual sacrifices, acceptable to God by Jesus Christ.

In order to build His church, He builds His people. As a believer, you are one of God's lively stones that He is using to build His church, His spiritual house. How does He do that?

Jesus basically told Peter that revelation had made him a rock. Likewise, you could say that revelation has made you a "lively stone." The truth is that revelation has solidified you; it has stabilized you.

God wants the body of Christ to increase and reach a place where the kingdom of God, or His church, is the dominant force on the planet (Daniel 2). That will happen, but in order for it to happen, God is going to have to build His church by building His people.

> Ephesians 2
> [19]Now therefore ye are no more strangers and foreigners, but fellowcitizens with the saints, and of the household of God;

[20]And are built upon the foundation of the apostles and prophets, Jesus Christ himself being the chief corner stone.

Paul is talking to believers. He is saying that the apostles and prophets are not only lively stones but also the foundation for the church. Jesus did not just teach the multitudes; He took time to live among the apostles and teach them with the intention of developing them into mature Christians who would be able to continue His work when He was gone. Thus, instead of one man doing the work of the Father, twelve men were doing the works of Jesus.

The apostles are not the only people with whom God wants to build His church. He wants His church growing, and it has been. But He is far from done. Some people feel that Jesus is returning soon and He is, but there may be more work to do and more time to accomplish this task than they think.

Some people say, "We've done our part. Let's lie back and wait for Jesus. He'll be here soon." Jesus told Christians to occupy until He comes (Luke 19:13). You need to keep working, keep doing your part in building His church, because He wants to use as many stones as He can.

James 5:7
Be patient therefore, brethren, unto the coming of the Lord. Behold, the husbandman waiteth for the precious fruit of the earth, and hath long patience for it, until he receive the early and latter rain.

God is waiting for the precious fruit of the earth. He is trying to win every soul that He can before Jesus returns, and even then He will keep building His church during the tribulation.

2 Timothy 3
¹⁶All Scripture is given by inspiration of God, and is profitable for doctrine, for reproof, for correction, for instruction in righteousness:
¹⁷That the man of God may be perfect, thoroughly furnished unto all good works.

The Greek word for "perfect" means "mature, of full age." God gave you the Word because it is His will that you are built up into a mature Christian, that you be a "lively stone" who will do good works of winning the lost, consolidating the found, discipling young believers, and sending them out to do the work of the ministry. That is how the body is built. But in order for God to build the body, He first has to build you. If He can get you to a place of maturity, then He knows you are equipped to go forth and build the body.

In John 12, Jesus speaks about His death and resurrection, the reason God had Him come.

John 12
²³And Jesus answered them, saying, The hour is come, that the Son of man should be glorified.
²⁴Verily, verily, I say unto you, Except a corn of wheat fall into the ground and die, it abideth alone: but if it die, it bringeth forth much fruit.

What does wheat bring forth? More wheat. Jesus, speaking of Himself, said that God was having Him die—He was going into the Earth—and God would raise Him again. Why? So that Jesus could bring forth fruit like Him, people who become like Jesus and help build His church.

Just like an architect needs a blueprint, a construction company, materials, and a timeline to construct a building, God has a strategy for building His church. In fact, He has had all these things in place from the beginning. Believers need to know God's plan so they can participate in building the body of Christ, in bringing about increase.

Empowerment

How did God set up His church to keep growing?

> Acts 1:8
> But ye shall receive power, after that the Holy Ghost is come upon you: and ye shall be witnesses unto me both in Jerusalem, and in all Judaea, and in Samaria, and unto the uttermost part of the earth.

When the Holy Ghost comes upon you, you receive power to be a witness. In this passage, the disciples, along with Mary, the other women and His brethren (about 120 individuals in all) were baptized in the Holy Ghost on the Day of Pentecost. They now had power to do the works of Jesus—to teach, preach, heal, deliver, and so on.

After that empowering, Peter preached the first message delivered under the anointing since Jesus' death and resurrection.

> Acts 2:41
> Then they that gladly received his word were baptized: and the same day there were added unto them about three thousand souls.

When Peter finished preaching, about 3,000 people were saved and baptized. They were added to the original 120, making about 3,120 people prepared to continue Jesus' work of building the church. One of the meanings of the Greek word for "added" is "annexed," which means that the church had more lively stones.

When you come out of the world into the body of Christ, you are a new creature spiritually. However, a new believer's thought process and actions may not necessarily have changed. He may still think the same way, and his flesh may still want to do the same things it did before becoming a Christian. His flesh is used to having its way.

New believers need to immerse themselves in the things of God so they can get free from sin and become the people God wants them to be, to really become like Jesus.

Perseverance

Look at the process in Acts 2:

> Acts 2:42
> And they continued stedfastly in the apostles' doctrine and fellowship, and in breaking of bread, and in prayers.

The Greek word for "steadfastly" means "to be earnest towards, to persevere, to be constantly diligent." In other words, the three thousand people did not get saved and then stop growing in the things of God.

Speaking as a pastor, I have not known many people who got saved and immediately became diligent about the things of God. That tells me that these people in Acts 2 must have had some help. The 120 believers must have stepped up, grabbed these new Christians, and told them what they should be doing—taught them doctrine (Matthew 28:20). They must have *"consider[ed] one another to provoke unto love and to good works" (Hebrews 10:24).*

They also must have continued in fellowship. When you first get saved, you have to leave your old friends behind. You need new friends, people in the faith.

> Proverbs 18:24
> A man that hath friends must shew himself friendly: and there is a friend that sticketh closer than a brother.

One mistake new believers make is to get angry because nobody is reaching out to them. Now, somebody should be reaching out to them, but even if no one does they need to show themselves to be friendly. These new believers in Acts 2 continued steadfastly in coming together and hanging out with the saints. They did not say, "I don't want to do this. I don't want to do that." They just persevered.

The *Amplified Bible* expands upon the phrase "breaking of bread" in Acts 2:42 by saying, *"the breaking of bread [including the Lord's Supper] and prayers."* Sometimes we think that the breaking of bread refers only to communion, but most commentaries say this phrase was used whenever believers came together and ate. Sitting down and having a meal with someone helps you get to know that person. You have to talk. Eating with someone opens the door to a relationship with that person.

Notice, also, that continuing *"in prayers"* was an essential component of growing in faith.

These new believers gave God the best year of their lives. They did not just get saved and say, "I have eternal life insurance now." No, they said, "I receive You, Jesus, as my Lord, and now I'm going to immerse myself into Your way." They allowed these 120 Christians to steer them into the lifestyle God wanted them to live—in doctrine, in fellowship, in breaking of bread, and in prayers. They were intent on becoming solid, mature Christians—the right away.

If you are a new believer, you need to give God the best year of your life. Don't play around with this. It should not take five, seven, or ten years before your life honors God. Your maturity is not necessarily based on time. It is based on how much revelation you receive. Revelation makes you like a rock.

Notice the next thing that happened according to Acts 2.

> Acts 2:46
> And they, continuing daily with one accord in the temple, and breaking bread from house to house, did eat their meat with gladness and singleness of heart.

These 3,120 believers focused daily on spiritual growth. Some folks think they are too busy for God, but these people had jobs and families, too. The difference was that any time that was not given to these responsibilities was used for God, not their own pleasure.

"With one accord" is a key phrase in this verse. In my years as a pastor, I have noticed that fellowship promotes unity. It helps people be *"with one accord."*

Not only did these people come together in the temple, but they also broke bread *"from house to house."* When God started the church, He did not simply set up Sunday and midweek meetings. He had His people going to services at church, but He also had them going from house to house; some translations say "in their homes."

These practices—fellowship, the breaking of bread, even the prayers—could not take place in the service. Those disciplines took place in the house. So if a believer skipped the house meeting, he or she missed out on receiving essential components for maturing and becoming like Jesus.

God's plan is still in place today. Believer, you cannot just go to the temple for fellowship, breaking of bread, and prayers of agreement. You, too, need to meet with other believers in a house.

The early church ate their meat with gladness and singleness of heart. They were a happy church.

> Acts 2:47
> ...praising God, and having favour with all the people. And the Lord added to the church daily such as should be saved.

God was building His church daily as they followed His plan for how the church as a whole was supposed to operate.

Signs and Wonders

In Acts 3, Peter and John were entering the Gate Beautiful when they saw a lame man asking for alms.

> Acts 3
> [6]Then Peter said, Silver and gold have I none; but such as I have give I thee: In the name of Jesus Christ of Nazareth rise up and walk.

⁷And he took him by the right hand, and lifted him up: and immediately his feet and ankle bones received strength.
⁸And he leaping up stood, and walked, and entered with them into the temple, walking, and leaping, and praising God.
⁹And all the people saw him walking and praising God:
¹⁰And they knew that it was he which sat for alms at the Beautiful gate of the temple: and they were filled with wonder and amazement at that which had happened unto him.

In this passage and others, we see that another master key to building the church is signs and wonders.

Mark 16
¹⁵And he said unto them, Go ye into all the world, and preach the gospel to every creature.
¹⁶He that believeth and is baptized shall be saved; but he that believeth not shall be damned.
¹⁷And these signs shall follow them that believe.

God's will is not that we witness without any signs. God's will is that things happen when we preach. Too many times we have the witnessing but we do not have the signs, so our success rate is lower than it should be.

Acts 4:4
Many of them which heard the word believed; and the number of the men was about five thousand.

As a result of all those people coming together, five thousand more people were saved, which meant that the church now numbered more than eight thousand.

> Acts 4:32
> And the multitude of them that believed were of one heart and of one soul: neither said any of them that ought of the things which he possessed was his own; but they had all things common.

In the natural, it is impossible to have that many people in one accord, but God's system results in unity.

The church continued to grow. In Acts 5, we read that there was a revival as a result of Peter and the apostles preaching, and signs and wonders manifesting.

> Acts 5:14
> And believers were the more added to the Lord, multitudes both of men and women.

As a result of the apostles having such success, the high priests (the authorities of the time)—in fact, some of the very ones who crucified Jesus—were angry.

> Acts 5:28
> ...saying, Did not we straitly command you that ye should not teach in this name? and, behold, ye have filled Jerusalem with your doctrine, and intend to bring this man's blood upon us.

How did the apostles *"fill Jerusalem with [this] doctrine"?* They did this in about a year, as a result of their services in the temple and from house to house, and as a result of being unified and witnessing with signs and wonders.

The high priests called in the leaders of the early Christian church and told them not to preach in the name of Jesus. These men were even beaten by the religious authorities.

> Acts 5:41
> And they departed from the presence of the council, rejoicing that they were counted worthy to suffer shame for his name.

These boys had grown up! When Jesus was first taken, the disciples ran away, but God had since matured them, and the Holy Ghost had empowered them.

> Acts 5:42
> Daily in the temple, and in every house, they ceased not to teach and preach Jesus Christ.

So they were not just preaching daily in the temple; they were preaching in every house. On a consistent basis, people were coming together in their homes and the apostles were teaching and preaching to them about Jesus .

God's will is that the church increase through ministry in the home, and His plan has not changed. The same dynamic is in place today. When believers do not meet from house to house, our success rate is lower than God wills it to be. Staff ministers from the church should be going to Touch Groups on a regular basis just to preach from their hearts. Today, God's church should be working His original plan for meeting and ministering together in houses.

> Acts 6:1a
> And in those days, when the number of the disciples was multiplied...

The number of believers multiplied. Notice this verse does notsay that the disciples doubled or even tripled; they had to have increased by a multiple of at least four, making the number of believers in the 30-35,000 range. All this growth happened because God's strategy was being followed.

Strife
When the church multiplied:

> Acts 6:1b
> ...there arose a murmuring of the Grecians against the Hebrews, because their widows were neglected in the daily ministration.

Where there is growth, satan will try to bring strife. Scripture says that we are not ignorant of his devices (2 Corinthians 2:11). Many times, when the church reaches a certain stage of growth, the people start talking, murmuring, and complaining. God has to stop the growth of the church and clean out the mess. Then, He can grow the church from there.

Too many times, people allow Satan to use them to bring about strife. Eventually they will allow Satan to push them out. But God will get rid of the little leaven that is leavening the lump (Galatians 5:9).

Ministry of Helps
In the early church, when strife arose:

> Acts 6
> ²Then the twelve called the multitude of the disciples unto them, and said, It is not reason that we should leave the word of God, and serve tables.
> ³Wherefore, brethren, look ye out among you seven men of honest report, full of the Holy Ghost and wisdom, whom we may appoint over this business.

The ministry of helps was birthed to keep the church growing. If the pastor had to do everything necessary to keep a church growing, he would not have time for any revelation. If you are not called to be an apostle, prophet, evangelist, pastor, or teacher, then you are called to be involved in the ministry of helps.

Notice that the ministry of helps came into the body of Christ long after house groups (what I call Touch Groups) did. It was never the will of God that the ministry of helps supplant the meetings in the houses. Some people think that because they serve in the ministry of helps they do not need to be involved in a small group. They need to renew their minds and stop rebelling against God's plan. God's plan has always been for believers to go from house to house as well as to the temple.

The church responded wholeheartedly to the disciples' plan.

> Acts 6:5
> And the saying pleased the whole multitude: and

they chose Stephen, a man full of faith and of the Holy Ghost, and Philip, and Prochorus, and Nicanor, and Timon, and Parmenas, and Nicolas a proselyte of Antioch.

They found seven men whose lifestyles testified to their faith—they were of honest report, full of the Holy Ghost, full of faith, and full of wisdom.

Now, remember that the church was barely two years old. That means that these people had not been in the church for years before they grew up. No, they matured to this point in less than two years. And the whole church—at least thirty thousand people—recognized their maturity.

The early church was not divided. They were able to make these selections because these men's lives were exemplary. They had grown in a short time because they followed God's plan. Winning the lost and doing signs and wonders—in the temple and from house to house—not only help you reach the lost but also helps develop you as a Christian.

> Acts 6:7
> And the word of God increased; and the number of the disciples multiplied in Jerusalem greatly; and a great company of the priests were obedient to the faith.

The church multiplied again. The events of Acts 6:8 occurred at least four years after the Day of Pentecost, so in this time span the church had grown to hundreds of thousands of believers. Why? Because they worked God's plan. If you want supernatural growth, you have to follow the plan. You have to minister to the people from house to house as well as in the temple.

Persecution

Acts 8 tells us that the next thing that happened with the early church involved persecution and that Saul was one of the individuals who led that persecution.

> Acts 8:3
> As for Saul, he made havock of the church, entering into every house, and haling men and women committed them to prison.

Saul did not persecute the church by entering into the temple and breaking up the meetings. No, he went from house to house and broke up the small-group meetings. Satan's first attack on the church occurred in the homes. The persecution ended when Saul, the key persecutor, got saved. Saul—now Paul—entered into his ministry.

In Acts 20, Paul was going to leave Ephesus, and he called for all the elders to come to him. This meeting with the elders was very similar to a small group.

> Acts 20
> [18]And when they were come to him, he said unto them, Ye know, from the first day that I came into Asia, after what manner I have been with you at all seasons,
> [19]Serving the Lord with all humility of mind, and with many tears, and temptations, which befell me by the lying in wait of the Jews:
> [20]And how I kept back nothing that was profitable unto you, but have shewed you, and have taught you publicly, and from house to house,

> ²¹Testifying both to the Jews, and also to the Greeks, repentance toward God, and faith toward our Lord Jesus Christ.

Paul stayed in Ephesus for two years, and he was able to reach the Jews and the Greeks. The gospel was preached in the whole area. But notice that Paul did not just preach to the multitudes; he also preached from house to house.

If you are not involved in a small group, do not be surprised that you are not growing. Do not be surprised if you are not experiencing the fullness of God. There are a number of things you will receive in a Touch Group meeting that you cannot get in a service, and this is why meeting from house to house is part of God's plan.

This system that God had in place would not have worked if the first 120 disciples had not stepped up and become involved in the lives of the early believers. People continued to get involved, because the church continued to multiply. Obviously, those who were born again grew spiritually themselves, and then stepped up and discipled other believers. They led groups.

If you are not directly involved in discipling believers, you are hurting the church. Being involved in some kind of church ministry is good, but it must not replace your responsibility to help new believers grow.

A Call to Men

In my experience as a pastor, I have observed that women are more inclined to get involved in Touch Groups than men. However, men, more than anyone, need the accountability of Touch Groups. We need to meet from house to house. Iron sharpens iron. Men sharpen men. Churches grow when men disciple one another. So step up to the plate and assume positions of leadership in discipling men. Work God's plan!

I am saddened when young brothers walk into my church and then walk out in the same condition because no other man is helping them apply what they have heard preached. It is good for a woman to try to reach out to a young man, but that does not have the same impact as when a man looks another man in the face and says, "Hey, brother, how are you doing?" Men of God, you need to step up. If you are too busy, your priorities are not in order.

In the early church, men discipled other men.

> Romans 16
> [3]Greet Priscilla and Aquila my helpers in Christ Jesus:
> [4]Who have for my life laid down their own necks: unto whom not only I give thanks, but also all the churches of the Gentiles.
> [5]Likewise greet the church that is in their house.

Priscilla and Aquila were Touch Group leaders. The church met in houses consistently, not only when Peter or Paul showed up.

In Colossians 4, Paul was an aged man, but he still said the same thing:

> Colossians 4:15
> Salute the brethren which are in Laodicea, and Nymphas, and the church which is in his house.

Nymphas (some translations say "Nympha," referring to a woman) was a Touch Group leader.

The home plays a big role in God's plan for the church, because for the church to grow, the individual believer must first be discipled. This occurs best in a small group.

> Philemon
> ¹Paul, a prisoner of Jesus Christ, and Timothy our brother, unto Philemon our dearly beloved, and fellowlabourer,
> ²And to our beloved Apphia, and Archippus our fellowsoldier, and to the church in thy house.

This is another Scripture that shows the church meeting not only in the temple, but also from house to house.

Thank God for the blueprint. We do not have to figure out how to make this thing work. It is written in the Word of God. All we have to do is follow the plan.

It Happened in a House

For insight into the plan, look at how Jesus fulfilled His ministry. He spent time with the multitudes, but many times He ministered in a home to a group of people, and supernatural things happened.

> Luke 5:17
> And it came to pass on a certain day, as he was teaching, that there were Pharisees and doctors of the law sitting by, which were come out of every town of Galilee, and Judaea, and Jerusalem: and the power of the Lord was present to heal them.

Mark 2 tells us that the place was so full that nobody could get in, even by the door. Jesus was ministering and teaching in a Touch Group. The power of God was present to heal in a house, not in a church or a healing conference. When Jesus was teaching, the anointing showed up in the house, and anyone who operated by faith received a healing.

Notice the next thing that happened.

> Luke 5
> [18] And, behold, men brought in a bed a man which was taken with a palsy: and they sought means to bring him in, and to lay him before him. [19] And when they could not find by what way they might bring him in because of the multitude, they went upon the housetop, and let him down through the tiling with his couch into the midst before Jesus.

Jesus began ministering to this man. Verse 25 tells us what happened.

> Luke 5:25
> And immediately he rose up before them, and took up that whereon he lay, and departed to his own house, glorifying God.

Again, this all happened *in a house*.

> Luke 4
> [38] And he arose out of the synagogue, and entered

into Simon's house. And Simon's wife's mother was taken with a great fever; and they besought him for her.
^{39}And he stood over her, and rebuked the fever; and it left her: and immediately she arose and ministered unto them.
^{40}Now when the sun was setting, all they that had any sick with divers diseases brought them unto him; and he laid his hands on every one of them, and healed them.

Jesus was once again in a house.

Luke 4:41
And devils also came out of many, crying out, and saying, Thou art Christ the Son of God. And he rebuking them suffered them not to speak: for they knew that he was Christ.

Mass healings and the rebuking of devils all happened in a house, not in a temple. In Luke 8, Jairus' daughter had died. Jesus took the anointing to Jairus's house, and the girl was raised from the dead.

Luke 8
^{51}And when he came into the house, he suffered no man to go in, save Peter, and James, and John, and the father and the mother of the maiden.
^{52}And all wept, and bewailed her: but he said, Weep not; she is not dead, but sleepeth.
^{53}And they laughed him to scorn, knowing that she was dead.

⁵⁴And he put them all out, and took her by the hand, and called, saying, Maid, arise.

I like the way Jesus dealt with those who scorned Him, don't you? He threw them out of the house!

Luke 8
⁵⁵And her spirit came again, and she arose straightway: and he commanded to give her meat.
⁵⁶And her parents were astonished: but he charged them that they should tell no man what was done.

The daughter was raised from the dead, but it wasn't during a Friday night prayer meeting or Sunday morning service. It happened in a house.

The power of God is in Touch Groups. This isn't man's system; it is God's plan. When you follow God's plan of ministering to people in homes, God's power shows up. And when God's power shows up, God's will is accomplished. People get revelation, they get healed, they get set free, and they get delivered. Their lives are never the same.

Luke 14
¹And it came to pass, as he went into the house of one of the chief Pharisees to eat bread on the sabbath day, that they watched him.
²And, behold, there was a certain man before him which had the dropsy.
³And Jesus answering spake unto the lawyers and Pharisees, saying, Is it lawful to heal on the sabbath day?

⁴And they held their peace. And he took him, and healed him, and let him go.

Again, this happened *in a house.*

After Jesus was resurrected, Scripture says that the apostles were all gathered in a house when Jesus walked through the wall. Thomas skipped Touch Group that day, and he missed this appearance. Don't be like Thomas. Don't miss an appearance of God because you did not show up.

God shows up in Touch Groups. So if you need more of God, go to a Touch Group. You can never have too much of God. God wants you filled with all of His fullness.

The Disciples Work the Plan

> Acts 2:1
> And when the day of Pentecost was fully come, they were all with one accord in one place.

This was a morning Touch Group. Nobody missed out on a move of God because everybody showed up.

> Acts 2
> ²And suddenly there came a sound from heaven as of a rushing mighty wind, and it filled all the house where they were sitting.
> ³And there appeared unto them cloven tongues like as of fire, and it sat upon each of them.

They all saw in the spirit realm—in a house!

Acts 2:4
And they were all filled with the Holy Ghost, and began to speak with other tongues, as the Spirit gave them utterance.

The outpouring of the Holy Ghost happened not in the temple, but in a house. Acts 9 says that when Saul saw Jesus on the road to Damascus, he was blinded because of the glory. God told Ananias to go to the house where Paul was. When Ananias walked in that house and laid hands on Paul, the scales came off his eyes. He was baptized in the Holy Ghost. Paul got set free and commissioned in a house, and he came to understand more of his calling in a house.

In Acts 10, we read that the Gentiles had not yet heard the gospel. It had been eleven years since Jesus came, died and rose again. Peter, while praying in a house, received wisdom from God that it was time to minister to the Gentiles. He went to Cornelius' house, and while preaching to Cornelius, his friends, and his family, the Holy Ghost came into the place. They were all filled with the Holy Ghost and speaking in other tongues.

In Acts 12, Peter was in prison. All the believers were praying without ceasing, and as they were praying together in their Touch Group, the breakthrough came. An angel showed up and brought Peter out of prison.

The end result of following God's plan for the church, which is not only meeting in the temple but meeting from house to house, is found in Acts 9.

Acts 9:31
Then had the churches rest throughout all Judaea and Galilee and Samaria, and were edified; and

walking in the fear of the Lord, and in the comfort of the Holy Ghost, were multiplied.

Notice how much the church had grown—throughout all Judaea, Galilee, and Samaria—in about six years. Multiplication is the will of God for the body of Christ. Multiplication is the will of God for our churches today. To get there, we have to follow God's plan, coming together not only in the temple, but also from house to house.

Chapter 2

Benefits of Small Group Involvement

The degree to which you will experience God's blessing is dependent upon the degree to which you follow His blueprint for growth. If you only come to church on Sunday mornings, you are not going to know the fullness of God's blessing. In order to live in God's best, you have to be involved in a Touch Group, because that is how He set up His system.

I was talking recently to a minister about Touch Groups when a rabbi said:

> Jewish people have been doing this for centuries. We have a gathering place for the community where women and men assemble for prayer and teaching. Married men teach other married men how to be good husbands, and wives teach other women how to be good wives. For example, if a woman does not know how to cook, other women will teach her.

When the rabbi said this, I immediately thought of Acts 2:42.

Acts 2:42
And they continued stedfastly in the apostles' doctrine and fellowship, and in breaking of bread, and in prayers.

When the Jews of Acts 2 became Christians, this practice of meeting in small groups was already part of their culture; they were only changing the curriculum and the people with whom they met.

When the Jews of Acts 2 became Christians, this practice of meeting in small groups was already part of their culture; they were only changing the curriculum and the people with whom they met.

Meeting in small groups is not part of our culture, which is why it is difficult for some people to become part of a Touch Group. Small groups are important to kingdom culture, however, so people who are newly saved need to have their minds renewed on this issue. When you are reaching out to people, you need to love them, pray for them, and patiently encourage them to get involved.

God desires for believers to come together in the temple, because there are things that can only be accomplished when we assemble in large groups. But there is also a reason God desires that believers meet from house to house. There are some things you can receive in a Touch Group that you cannot receive in a temple.

I like to use the following analogy. Some people take vitamins and supplements because they do not receive all the nutrients they need in their daily diet. They may be deficient in one area or another. In fact, if they do not take supplements, over a period of time they will reap the consequence of that deficiency; they will not be as healthy as they otherwise might be.

Your Touch Group is your spiritual vitamin supplement. If you do not participate in a small group, you will be deficient in the areas of spiritual growth that Touch Groups facilitate. It will be difficult for you to be a complete, healthy Christian.

The body of Christ has had difficulty producing mature Christians. Too many people go through years of battle when spiritual growth need not have taken that long.

The enemy of great is good. Too many people are satisfied with being good at something without striving to reach their full potential. They never experience greatness because they are satisfied with being good. If you are not participating in a Touch Group ministry, you are sacrificing your potential for a great Christian life.

Let's look at several reasons why we need Touch Groups.

Small Groups Promote Fellowship

> Acts 2:42
> And they continued stedfastly in the apostles' doctrine and fellowship, and in breaking of bread, and in prayers.

The first reason Christians need Touch Groups is that small groups promote fellowship. The early believers were diligent in fellowship. The Greek word for "fellowship" is *koinonia*, meaning "partnership, participation, social intercourse, and communion with other believers."

Humans are social beings. Even introverted people need fellowship, and most have it, just with fewer people than extroverts have in their lives. You are going to hang out with someone, and that person is going to have a great impact on how you live your life.

> 2 Corinthians 6:14
> Be ye not unequally yoked together with unbelievers: for what fellowship hath righteousness with unrighteousness? and what communion hath light with darkness?

The Greek word for "yoked" means "a strong bond." If you are a believer, you should not have strong emotional bonds with unbelievers. Non-Christians should not be your hanging buddies. You should not be going to the movies with them or going to bars with them.

Believers should have strong bonds with their brothers and sisters in the Lord. Saints should hang out with other saints. Christian men, in particular, are often loners or hang out with sinners. Too often Christian men do not spend much time together. A Christian man needs male friends who are saved, filled with the Holy Ghost, and living the Word of God to help him stay on track.

> Psalm 1:1
> Blessed is the man that walketh not in the counsel of the ungodly, nor standeth in the way of sinners, nor sitteth in the seat of the scornful.

God does not take something away without giving us a better replacement. If you are not to walk in the counsel of the ungodly, what are you to do? You are supposed to stand in the way of believers. You are supposed to sit in the seat of those who are serving God.

When the three thousand people became Christians in Acts 1, the 120 older believers did not say, "Thank God you are saved, but we don't want you to come over here and join us." No, they had not formed a clique.

Too many churches have factions that do not make new believers feel welcome. These older believers have been hanging together for years, and it is easy for them to say, "You just became a Christian? That's great! But you are still cussing a bit, so get away from me."

One reason young believers do not fellowship with the saints, and consequently end up back with people in the world, is that people in the world accept folks the way they are. Scripture says that older believers should be teaching younger believers the things of the Word of God. You cannot do that if you never allow them to come near you or talk to you.

Where can you get this kind of fellowship? Look at what the Scriptures say Acts 2.

> Acts 2:46
> And they, continuing daily with one accord in the temple, and breaking bread from house to house, did eat their meat with gladness and singleness of heart.

There is no better way to experience fellowship than to walk into someone's house and sit down and talk about things. You can have some chat time in a foyer after service, but that venue does not really foster deep fellowship, especially if you attend a church that has two or three services on Sunday. The main reason you go to church on Sunday is for worship, not for fellowship. But fellowship is one of the main purposes for being involved in a Touch Group.

> Colossians 3:13
> Forbearing one another, and forgiving one another, if any man have a quarrel against any: even as Christ forgave you, so also do ye.

Once in a while people are going to say things or do things they are not supposed to do. But we should not put our fellow believers on a pedestal. Do not threaten to leave the church or Touch Group just because one of your brothers or sisters messes up.

Christians are family. When a family member is in trouble, the rest of the family does not give up on him. They come together to deal with the situation. Believers should do the same thing. We need one another.

Small Groups Promote Accountability

The second reason Christians need Touch Groups is that small groups promote accountability.

> Hebrews 10:24
> And let us consider one another to provoke unto love and to good works.

The *Amplified Bible* says:

> And let us consider and give attentive, continuous care to watching over one another, studying how we may stir up (stimulate and incite) to love and helpful deeds and noble activities.

Ephesians 6:18 is similar.

Ephesians 6:18
Praying always with all prayer and supplication in the Spirit, and watching thereunto with all perseverance and supplication for all saints.

We Christians are not just supposed to look at our own lives; we are also to be watching the lives of our fellow believers. We need to know what's going on in their lives so we know when and how to pray for them.

Some Christians never get past thinking about themselves. But God says we should be just as concerned about our brothers and sisters as we are about ourselves.

One of the Touch Groups in the church I pastor supported a member and her young children when her husband went overseas. They were a great blessing to her. This is how it is supposed to work. We Christians need one another. When we need help, we should run to a fellow believer for help, not to a sinner or a secular organization.

The Greek word for "provoke" in Hebrews 10:24 means to "incite to good." Christians should not be looking at one anothers' lives in order to gossip. We should be trying to figure out how we can help each other do what God told us to do— to love. Love encompasses everything we are supposed to do as believers. The Bible says love is the fulfillment of the law.

Romans 13
[8]Owe no man any thing, but to love one another: for he that loveth another hath fulfilled the law.
[9]For this, Thou shalt not commit adultery, Thou halt not kill, Thou shalt not steal, Thou shalt not bear false witness, Thou shalt not covet; and if there be any other commandment, it is briefly

comprehended in this saying, namely, Thou shalt love thy neighbour as thyself.

¹⁰Love worketh no ill to his neighbour: therefore love is the fulfilling of the law.

If I am *provoking* my brother to love, I am checking up on him, talking to him, and helping him live a Christian life. If he's dating someone, I might ask, "Are you having a hard time staying pure? Let me help you by telling you how God helped me." If he is having any issues, I am there for him.

One reason believers slip is because they do not have anyone to whom they answer. The pastor cannot be personally involved in the life of each member of his church. Every believer is responsible for provoking other believers in the Christian life.

Proverbs 27:17
Iron sharpeneth iron; so a man sharpeneth the countenance of his friend.

Believers keep one another sharp. Men keep men sharp. Women keep women sharp. You need to be sharp spiritually to be successful in this life.

If you do not have that kind of relationship with another believer, if you have not allowed yourself to be accountable to someone, you are not working the system God set up to help you grow as a Christian. If you are too proud to admit that you have a problem, you are a dull Christian. Dull Christians are not successful Christians. Sharp Christians are successful Christians. That brother who is in your face, who loves you and stays involved in your life, that brother who sees you at every Touch Group meeting, helps to keep you accountable. He provides an example of a sharp Christian.

In John 13, Jesus had just finished washing the feet of His disciples when He said:

> John 13:15
> For I have given you an example, that ye should do as I have done to you.

Jesus' life was a powerful example to those apostles. They were with Him all the time. They saw everything He did—how He got up, how He interacted with others, how He lived His life. Because of that example, when He left, the disciples acted just like Jesus.

Jesus did not do a lot of training on the works of the ministry; He mainly told the disciples to *do* the work of the ministry. How did they know how to proceed? They had seen Him do it. Modeling is one of the most effective methods of teaching.

In one of the Touch Groups in the church I pastor, a woman stopped the study and said, with tears in her eyes, "Every time I come here, I feel like everyone is living for God but me. I want what you all have." The Touch Group members gathered around her and prayed until she was filled with the Holy Ghost.

When you are around people who are modeling the life of Jesus, you can see how this life can be lived. If all you do is go to church on Sunday mornings, and all you see is the pastor who is living like Jesus, it is easy to say, "Well, that's his job." But when you see other believers on a regular basis who have the same type of job you have and are living like Jesus, there is power in that example.

Being around men of God sharpens me. Whenever they start talking about the things of God, I think, *I have work to do! I have to be as sharp spiritually as they are!* That's iron sharpening iron!

There is power in an example. Godly associations bring increase; ungodly associations bring decrease. The Bible says that if you run with riotous men you will get their destruction. That tells me that if I run with righteous men, I will get their prosperity.

There is a time and place for minding your own business, but there is also a time and place to get involved in the lives of others.

> Hebrews 3:12
> Take heed, brethren, lest there be in any of you an evil heart of unbelief, in departing from the living God.

Paul is not talking to pastors here; he's talking to all believers. In essence, he's saying, "Watch out for one another, and if you see somebody starting to stray from God's path, help him get back on."

> Hebrews 3:13
> But exhort one another daily, while it is called To day; lest any of you be hardened through the deceitfulness of sin.

You need Touch Groups because you need accountability. If nobody's telling you what to do, I can guarantee your life is destruction. If no one is checking you in any way, your life is not going too well. You may think you are doing okay, but when you look at your life from God's perspective, you will see that you are far from the path.

Men are notorious for running from accountability. Now, I am not a big guy; there is nothing intimidating about me. But it is amazing how many men in the church I pastor are afraid of me. When a woman schedules a time for marital counseling, her husband often does not show up. If he comes once, he usually does not return. Why? Because he does not want to be held accountable. It takes a real man to say, "I have something I need to work on. Tell me when I'm messing up."

Let's look at several other Scriptures that talk about holding others accountable.

> Romans 15:14
> And I myself also am persuaded of you, my brethren, that ye also are full of goodness, filled with all knowledge, able also to admonish one another.

Christians are responsible for admonishing other Christians who are falling into sin.

> 2 Thessalonians 3:14
> And if any man obey not our word by this epistle, note that man, and have no company with him, that he may be ashamed.

In other words, Christian, do not hang out with people living in sin.

> 1 Corinthians 5
> [10]Yet not altogether with the fornicators of this world, or with the covetous, or extortioners, or with idolaters; for then must ye needs go out of the world.

> ¹¹But now I have written unto you not to keep company, if any man that is called a brother be a fornicator, or covetous, or an idolator, or a railer, or a drunkard, or an extortioner; with such an one no not to eat.

If a man is living in sin, do not even eat with him.

> 2 Thessalonians 3:15
> Yet count him not as an enemy, but admonish him as a brother.

Tell the fallen Christian he is missing it and help him get right. Admonish each other. Sharpen each other. Be accountable to each other.

When you come to church and there are thousands of people assembled on Sunday morning, no one is holding you accountable. There are some young men in the church whom I try to hold accountable to some things, so I tell them to make sure they see me when they come to church. But if they don't, I usually cannot find them in the crowd.

You find accountability in Touch Groups when you get to know people and they get to know you, when you all love one another and model godly lives.

> Acts 6:5
> And the saying pleased the whole multitude: and they chose Stephen, a man full of faith and of the Holy Ghost, and Philip, and Prochorus, and Nicanor, and Timon, and Parmenas, and Nicolas a proselyte of Antioch.

At this point, the early church was somewhere between one and two years old. They needed seven individuals to serve, men of honest report and full of the Holy Ghost. How did these men get to this point of maturity in just two years? How did they become so full of the Holy Ghost, faith, and wisdom that the people were able to look at their lives and elect them to be deacons?

They were obviously discipled. Someone had taken these new believers and showed them what they should and should not do. Somebody taught them how to pray and how to study God's Word. When people get saved at the church I pastor, we give them Bibles and tell them to start reading in the book of John. But there is only so much we can say, only so much information we can give them.

Where are the people who will teach them to pray? Where will this new Christian have an opportunity to pray in public for the first time? Where will this new Christian read Scripture and then report what he or she believes the Word says? In Touch Groups, that's where!

Christians have to hold one another accountable for spiritual growth. They have to provoke one another to good works such as serving, soul-winning, discipling other believers, praying, sowing, and giving.

Small Groups Promote Encouragement

The third reason Christians need Touch Groups is that small groups promote encouragement. There are times when you are standing in faith, but your situation is getting tough and you need encouragement. You need someone to help your faith stay strong. You need somebody to come alongside you and say, "Remember what you believe. Remember what God said. God has never failed you."

When we live without one another, it is easy for satan to

pick us off one at a time. It makes no sense to split up. There is strength in unity. There is strength in staying together.

Jude talks about individuals who were believers but strayed from the things of God and are now mockers. Look at how they are described:

> Jude 1:19
> These be they who separate themselves, sensual, having not the Spirit.

When you fail to come together with other believers, when you separate yourself, the next step is becoming fleshly, sensual. You are on your own, and Satan is picking you off.

> Hebrews 10:25
> Not forsaking the assembling of ourselves together, as the manner of some is; but exhorting one another: and so much the more, as ye see the day approaching.

Although it is important for Christians to attend church services, Paul is not necessarily talking just services here. You cannot provoke to love and good work in church services. You do that when you meet from house to house.

Don't skip Touch Group meetings. If you become Touch Group deficient, you are fellowship deficient, accountability deficient, and encouragement deficient. You will struggle, and when you are struggling, it is impossible for you to help someone else who is struggling.

The Greek word for "exhort" means "to call near, to invoke." It is translated elsewhere in Scripture as "to comfort." We should be exhorting other believers to good works, exhorting them to love. We should be comforting them and encouraging them to do what they are supposed to do.

> 1 Thessalonians 5:11
> Wherefore comfort yourselves together, and edify one another, even as also ye do.

To edify means to build up, which includes encouraging. In Acts 27, Paul was on a ship that was about to be shipwrecked, and he encouraged the sailors on the ship, saying, "Be of good cheer! We're not going to lose our lives" (Acts 27:22).

There are times when people are in the middle of a storm and they need to hear someone say, "Don't worry. God's going to bring you through this." Although you cannot get to a staff minister right away, you can always get to your Touch Group. They can encourage you, and they can get you fired up. They can pray with you, and they can edify you. We all need that.

Small Groups Promote Understanding of the Word

The fourth reason Christians need Touch Groups is that we need a greater understanding of the Word. One of the key facets of Touch Groups is studying the Word of God. In Touch Groups, you have a chance to talk about the message you heard last week or about the message you just read.

Matthew 13 and Mark 4 tell how satan works to keep the Word from taking root in our hearts. God will sow the Word, but one group of people does not receive it. Another group receives it with joy, but because the Word has no root, no depth, satan uproots that Word by sending trouble their way. Sometimes that happens because people do not open their hearts fully to receive the Word. But it also happens when people do not meditate on the Word they have received. Faith comes by hearing, and hearing comes by the Word of God.

Touch Groups facilitate that. They give people a chance to talk about the Word and look at it again and again. That Word that was shallow in your heart, which you were happy to hear, has a chance to get rooted. Now, it abides in you. It dwells in you richly.

In Touch Groups, not only do you read and hear the Word repeatedly, but also you get to speak the Word yourself, and that is one of the best ways to get the Word rooted. Once you start talking about what God has said, the Word moves deeper into your heart. Sunday morning services do not lend themselves to a question-and-answer format, but you can do that in a Touch Group. This type of session will result in a greater understanding of the Word.

Small Groups Promote Corporate Prayer

The fifth reason Christians need Touch Groups is they allow time for corporate prayer. The Bible talks about the prayer of agreement in Matthew 18.

> Matthew 18:19
> Again I say unto you, That if two of you shall agree on earth as touching any thing that they shall ask, it shall be done for them of my Father which is in heaven.

On Sunday mornings, corporate prayer usually focuses on understanding the Word of God and agreeing to hear it. We usually do not have time to pray about individual needs, but in a Touch Group you have plenty of time for prayer. Your faith may not be on a level to receive God's blessings on the basis of your own prayers, but when you hear yourself and other believers agree in prayer, your faith becomes strong enough to receive.

In Acts 4, when Peter and John were threatened, the Bible says they went back to their own company and all prayed together. In Acts 12, when Peter was put in prison, they came together in a house and prayed. People have had many breakthroughs in their lives because of corporate prayer in a Touch Group.

Chapter 3

The Call to Disciple Others

In a Touch Group you receive all the benefits of family, of being with your brothers and sisters in the Lord. Being part of a small group is the way to put fellowship, accountability, encouragement, the Word, and corporate prayer into your walk with God.

Touch Group participation not only helps you become strong in these areas, but also helps make you a mature believer who is able to help disciple others.

In Matthew 28, Jesus had been resurrected and was about to ascend into heaven when He spoke to the eleven disciples. His words are commonly referred to as the Great Commission. Christians are to love God and love others, but the major command Jesus delivered after He rose again was in this commission. In fact, this is the first command of the church age. If you do not carry out the Great Commission, you cannot expect to be blessed.

> Matthew 28
> [18]And Jesus came and spake unto them, saying, All power is given unto me in heaven and in earth.

¹⁹Go ye therefore, and teach all nations, baptizing them in the name of the Father, and of the Son, and of the Holy Ghost.

Jesus says, "I have all the authority, but I want you to go." Thus, you are able to fulfill that command only as you go in the authority of Jesus, in the name of Jesus.

This command was not just for the eleven disciples who were with Jesus at that moment, because there was no way those eleven could go into all nations. Although we have access to much greater technology than they did, it would still be difficult, if not impossible, for eleven people to go to all nations in their lifetime.

This command applies to everyone who has made Jesus Lord of his or her life. We all are supposed to "go." Not only are we commanded to go, we are also all commanded to teach. The Greek word for "teach" means "to become a pupil, to disciple, to enroll as scholar."

God said to make disciples, not converts. Too many times Christians make converts without making disciples. We convince sinners to pray the prayer of salvation and receive Jesus. They may have a moment or two where they try to walk in the things of God, but because they do not have help, provocation to love and good works, and discipling, they return to living the way they used to live. The Bible says they are worse off than they would have been if they had never known Jesus (2 Peter 2:21).

In fact, this nation is full of backslidden Christians. If the body of Christ could just reach the backslidden Christians, we would not have churches big enough to hold them. The reason we have so many backslidden Christians is that we have not followed God's blueprint for the church. We do not have meetings from house to house; we aren't discipling people.

Why? Too often we do not realize the fullness of what Jesus commanded us to do.

Jesus was not just saying, "Make converts." He was saying, "I want you to go out to all nations and cause them to become true followers of Me. Enroll them as scholars. Put them in the school of the Holy Ghost."

Baptize

Young's Literal Translation of the Holy Bible says:

> Matthew 28
> [18]And having come near, Jesus spake to them, saying, "Given to me was all authority in heaven and on earth;
> [19]having gone, then, disciple all the nations, (baptizing them—to the name of the Father, and of the Son, and of the Holy Spirit,
> [20]teaching them to observe all, whatever I did command you,) and lo, I am with you all the days—till the full end of the age."

This translation helps illustrate that discipling is inclusive of baptizing and teaching. In order to disciple someone, you must first baptize him, and then teach him.

Water baptism does not save a person, but it is an important moment in the life of a new believer. It is when he shows the world that when Jesus died, he died, and when Jesus rose, he rose. It shows the world that his old being is now dead and he is a new creature in Christ Jesus. Water baptism is a great method to *consolidate* new believers.

In the church I pastor, our mission is "to win, consolidate, disciple, and send." You will notice that the word *consolidate* comes in the middle. We do this because we're following God's blueprint. When Paul went on his missionary journeys and got people saved, instead of going to new cities where people hadn't heard the gospel, he he stayed and made sure they were established in the faith. He did not want to return only to minister to backslidden Christians.

Mike Tyson was once born again, but when he ran into trouble, no believer was there to help pick him up. He was not consolidated and discipled as a Christian. So when the Muslims gave him that type of attention, he converted to Islam.

Before a new believer gets out of the church, satan is already talking to him, saying, "You are not really saved because you are still thinking this and saying that." But he is saved. He just needs someone to minister to him so that he stays in the things of God and does not walk away from his decision.

One of the great methods of confirming a new believer's decision is to get him or her water baptized. In Acts, people got baptized immediately after being saved. That was the first step to making them disciples, to helping them grow up in God.

Teach

Another step toward making true disciples who follow Christ is to teach them. Another word for "teach" is *disciple*. As a believer, you are to teach the younger believers the things of God. Jesus says, "teaching them to observe [to do] all things whatsoever I have commanded you" (Matthew 28:20).

In essence, Jesus is saying, "I want you, Believer, to be involved in teaching other believers my Word." He's not necessarily talking about you getting up in a pulpit and preaching. He's talking about teaching people in the course of your everyday life.

In order to teach someone, you must first know the subject matter yourself. One minister said, "You can't deliver what you haven't received." You first need to have heard what God has said and taught. You are not to teach merely tradition or theory about the things of God.

In addition to having a mastery of the things He taught, you need to be living those truths. You cannot teach something effectively if you are not living it. As a parent, you cannot tell your child one thing and then do the opposite. Your child may hear what you are saying, but he will do what you are doing.

A leader can cause people to walk in righteousness, or he can cause people to walk in sin, based on how the leader himself lives his life. To help other people grow, we first need to grow spiritually ourselves.

God's Plan for Your Spiritual Growth

In 1 Peter 2, Peter told believers that they had been redeemed by the blood of the Lamb and born again through the Word of God, the incorruptible seed (1 Peter 1:18,19, 23). He reviewed the basics of salvation, then delivered another basic truth about spiritual growth.

> 1 Peter 2:2
> As newborn babes, desire the sincere milk
> of the word, that ye may grow thereby.

A newborn baby does nothing but eat, sleep, and cry—and lie there and look cute. She does not care what time it is when she is hungry. She wakes up screaming because she wants milk with all her being.

When was the last time you woke up screaming because you wanted the Word? Peter says we need to be like newborn babes. We need to desire the Word. The Greek word for "desire" means "to dote upon, to intensely crave possession." If you are desiring the Word, you will never skip church or a Touch Group meeting, because you crave the truth.

We understand what it means to intensely desire something in other contexts. Sports fans who want to attend a big game will line up and sleep outside the ticket center all night because they just have to have those tickets.

In other parts of the world, we see examples of people who intensely desire the Word. One minister said recently that he has preached in places where people have walked five miles to hear the Word and stayed in a tent in 120-degree weather for three days for the privilege of hearing a man of God preach. We are spoiled in the United States. If the air conditioner is not working at church, many people will not attend services.

It is important to God that you intensely crave the Word. He has a plan for your spiritual growth. He says, *"Desire the sincere milk of the word, that ye may grow thereby" (1 Peter 2:2).*

When you are born again, you are not a mature, fully developed Christian. You come into this new world as a spiritual babe. The more you get the Word, the more you grow spiritually. Just as a newborn babe experiences no growth without milk, newborn Christians experience no spiritual growth without the Word. Some people think they are growing spiritually just because time has passed, but if they are not getting the Word, they are not growing.

It is not enough for a newborn baby to be in the presence of milk; she needs to drink it, to receive it into her body. That is true concerning the Word of God also. You do not grow just because you come to church and hear the Word; you also need to receive it.

If a baby receives milk but keeps throwing it up, she has a problem. Likewise, if you do not do what is necessary to keep the Word in you, if you allow satan to prevent the Word from taking root and bearing fruit, if you allow the devil to keep the Word from abiding in you, then you have a spiritual problem.

God is trying to accomplish your spiritual growth. Second Timothy 3 says that the Word of God was given to us so that believers could be perfect.

> 2 Timothy 3
> ¹⁶All scripture is given by inspiration of God, and is profitable for doctrine, for reproof, for correction, for instruction in righteousness:
> ¹⁷That the man of God may be perfect, thoroughly furnished unto all good works.

The Greek word for "perfect" means "mature, of full age." Every time I receive the Word, it causes me to grow up a little bit more. Eventually, I will grow to a place of maturity.

> Ephesians 4:11
> And he gave some, apostles; and some, prophets; and some, evangelists; and some, pastors and teachers.

God gave five types of ministry gifts, or five anointings. Why?

> Ephesians 4:12
> For the perfecting of the saints, for the work of the ministry, for the edifying of the body of Christ.

These gifts are one reason we have church. A church service is an extension of the pastor's ministry. But every believer should be receiving from all these gifts. That is why it is good for you to partner with other ministries when God leads you to do so.

The Greek word for "perfecting" means "complete furnishing or equipping," which implies that a newborn Christian is not completely equipped. God's plan is to grow saints.

> Ephesians 4:15
> But speaking the truth in love, may grow up into him in all things, which is the head, even Christ.

Christians are to be growing up into the image of Jesus, growing spiritually until we look like Him. A spiritually mature man looks like Jesus.

Back up to verses 13 and 14.

> Ephesians 4
> [13]...till we all come in the unity of the faith, and of the knowledge of the Son of God, unto a perfect man, unto the measure of the stature of the fulness of Christ:
> [14]That we henceforth be no more children, tossed to and fro, and carried about with every wind of doctrine, by the sleight of men, and cunning craftiness, whereby they lie in wait to deceive.

God gave ministry gifts so the recipients of the gifts can help others get the Word. As you hear, receive, and abide in the Word, you keep growing until you reach the point of being a mature believer, a "thoroughly furnished" man or woman of God.

God gives children parents so the parents can train their children, naturally and spiritually, to be mature adults, assets to society and mighty seeds for God. If you are not raising that type of child, you are not fulfilling your mission as a parent. Every time you have a child you are taking on a mission.

Let's go a step further with this. We have established that God wants you to grow. He has given you the Word to grow, He has given you ministry gifts to grow, and His ultimate goal is that you grow up into a perfect man, a mature Christian. But there is something else you need to understand about God's plan for your spiritual growth. In James 1, the Bible teaches that the man who is perfect, mature, and entire is a man who lacks nothing.

> James 1:4
> But let patience have her perfect work, that ye may be perfect and entire, wanting nothing.

The mature Christian is blessed in every area of life. He walks in faith and love, health, prosperity, and safety—all the things in which God has planned for you to walk. Becoming a mature Christian is of great benefit, because it puts you in a position to prosper in every area of life. Therefore, focus on your spiritual growth, making it the highest priority.

If you are not growing spiritually, something is wrong. You are not supposed to stay the same spiritual age for five, ten, or thirty years.

Blessed in Order to Bless

The mature Christian does not grow up spiritually just so he can be blessed. God's plan is that you grow up spiritually so that you are a blessing to others.

Too many Christians stop at being blessed. They come to church, they keep getting the Word, they keep getting fed, but they are basically just fat sheep. They are not spiritually healthy, because mature Christians cannot keep taking in the Word without giving.

If you are naturally overweight and you stay that way long enough, you will start seeing the results in your body. Likewise, if you are spiritually overweight, you will start seeing the results of that in your life because you haven't done what God requires of you. You have not lived out the reason God wanted you to become spiritually mature.

> John 15:16
> Ye have not chosen me, but I have chosen you, and ordained you, that ye should go and bring forth fruit, and that your fruit should remain: that whatsoever ye shall ask of the Father in my name, he may give it you.

God chose you! It does not matter who you are or where you came from. God ordained you, which means that He appointed you or placed you in a particular position for a purpose.

Why did God choose you? Why did He place you where He did? God did all these things so that you could *"go and bring forth fruit."*

When you first get saved, you are the fruit. But as you grow and mature, you are to produce more fruit for God. Look at John 15 again:

> John 15
> ¹I am the true vine, and my Father is the husbandman.

²Every branch in me that beareth not fruit he taketh away: and every branch that beareth fruit, he purgeth it, that it may bring forth more fruit.

He is the vine, and you are the branch. If you do not bear fruit, you will be taken away, dishonorably discharged from duty. Sometimes we forget how important it is to God that we bear fruit.

When you do produce fruit, God says, "Good job! But let me clean you up a little bit more, let me grow you up a little bit more, so you can go bear even more fruit." God is greedy for fruit.

What kind of fruit is God waiting for?

> James 5:7
> Be patient therefore, brethren, unto the coming of the Lord. Behold, the husbandman waiteth for the precious fruit of the earth, and hath long patience for it, until he receive the early and latter rain.

God is greedy for souls, so He says, "I want you to bring forth even more fruit."

> John 15:3
> Now ye are clean through the word which I have spoken unto you.

In essence, He says, "I have given you the Word. I have already cleaned you up some. I have already grown you up some. But I expect you to go forward and start doing something."

> John 15:4
> Abide in me, and I in you. As the branch cannot bear fruit of itself, except it abide in the vine; no more can ye, except ye abide in me.

Christians have to abide in Him to bring forth fruit.

> John 15:8
> Herein is my Father glorified, that ye bear much fruit; so shall ye be my disciples.

If you are His disciple, then you are like Him. A true disciple is one who brings forth fruit, one who helps others become true disciples of God. It is not enough for you to get the Word and grow a little bit. It is not enough to get to a place where you feel you are furnished. Only when you bring forth fruit are you truly fulfilling God's purpose for your spiritual growth.

> John 15:16
> Ye have not chosen me, but I have chosen you, and ordained you, that ye should go and bring forth fruit, and that your fruit should remain: that whatsoever ye shall ask of the Father in my name, he may give it you.

Jesus is saying, "I want you to go bring forth fruit, to get people saved. But hold on—I don't want you just to get them converted. I want them to remain. I'm expecting you to make sure they're established in the things of God."

Do you remember what He said in verse 2?

John 15:2
Every branch in me that beareth not fruit he taketh away: and every branch that beareth fruit, he purgeth it, that it may bring forth more fruit.

You will remain only when you are bringing forth fruit. Your fruit will remain only when the people you have discipled bring forth fruit.
Look at Ephesians 4:12 again:

Ephesians 4:12
For the perfecting of the saints, for the work of the ministry, for the edifying of the body of Christ...

The *Amplified Bible* says:

Ephesians 4:12
His intention was the perfecting and the full equipping of the saints (His consecrated people), [that they should do] the work of ministering toward building up Christ's body (the church).

God is saying, "I gave you ministry gifts so you could grow up and do the work of the ministry, so that you could help build My church." Every believer is not only a stone in the temple of the body of Christ, but also responsible for helping place other stones in the temple of the body of Christ. What good is it to train a soldier who never goes into the field and fights? God's plan for your life is that you not only become mature, but that you bring forth fruit for Him by preaching to the lost and discipling the found until they have become true disciples.

In Hebrews 5, Paul says of Jesus:

> Hebrews 5
> [10]...called of God an high priest after the order of Melchisedec.
> [11]Of whom we have many things to say, and hard to be uttered, seeing ye are dull of hearing.

Paul is saying, "I have got some things to tell you about Melchisedec and about Jesus, but you are sluggish of hearing, lazy of hearing." How does he know this? Because of the results.

> Hebrews 5:12
> For when for the time ye ought to be teachers, ye have need that one teach you again which be the first principles of the oracles of God; and are become such as have need of milk, and not of strong meat.

The *Amplified Bible* says:

> Hebrews 5:12
> For even though by this time you ought to be teaching others, you actually need someone to teach you over again the very first principles of God's Word. You have come to need milk, not solid food.

The Call to Disciple Others

Paul is writing to believers, not to preachers. From God's viewpoint, the time should come when you are teaching others. God has you on a clock, spiritually speaking, and if you do not grow and begin to bring forth fruit, you will hear Him say, "I invested in you, and I expect a return."

The Greek word for "ought" means "to owe, to be under obligation, and to fail in duty." Paul is saying, "You have failed in your duty; by now you should be teachers. By now, you should be leading others."

A child who is in first grade is expected to enter second grade at the end of nine months, and he is expected to enter third grade after another nine-month period. Likewise, God has us on a schedule. He expects us to grow up faster than we may think He does.

In the church I pastor, we have a program called the Path to Leadership (see Appendix) that is designed to help new believers become mature Christians. The first step is a pre-encounter class, where believers are taught the first principles of Christ. The second step is an encounter, where believers are set free. The third step is a post-encounter, where believers are taught how to live their lives as Christians. We start with the basics, then teach leadership principles so believers can learn to live and lead like Jesus.

The Path to Leadership consists of ninety classes. Diligent students can complete this program in six months. Those who finish it are full of the Word and well equipped to lead and disciple others.

The key to growth is ministering to others. Teaching what you have learned makes you master the subject, and that makes you grow. If you never have to act on what you have learned, you may lose what you have learned. When you use it, you will not forget it.

Luke 12:42
And the Lord said, Who then is that faithful and wise steward, whom his lord shall make ruler over his household, to give them their portion of meat in due season?

A steward is someone who has been given something and is supposed to do something with it. God's Word has been given to you freely; you have received it freely. You are now to give it freely.

Luke 12
⁴³Blessed is that servant, whom his lord when he cometh shall find so doing.
⁴⁴Of a truth I say unto you, that he will make him ruler over all that he hath.
⁴⁵But and if that servant say in his heart, My lord delayeth his coming; and shall begin to beat the menservants and maidens, and to eat and drink, and to be drunken;
⁴⁶The lord of that servant will come in a day when he looketh not for him, and at an hour when he is not aware, and will cut him in sunder, and will appoint him his portion with the unbelievers.
⁴⁷And that servant, which knew his lord's will, and prepared not himself, neither did according to his will, shall be beaten with many stripes.
⁴⁸But he that knew not, and did commit things worthy of stripes, shall be beaten with few stripes. For unto whomsoever much is given, of him shall be much required: and to whom men have committed much, of him they will ask the more.

You have been given much. God will hold you accountable for that. If you have been disobedient to His command to disciple, He will hold you accountable for all the lives that were not impacted. Your calling is not about you. It is about others.

If you fulfill your calling, you will be blessed. And you will enjoy it, because God knows you well enough to know what you enjoy most. God's will is that His children grow up spiritually to a place where they will bring in more fruit for Him.

> 2 Timothy 2
> ¹Thou therefore, my son, be strong in the grace that is in Christ Jesus.
> ²And the things that thou hast heard of me among many witnesses, the same commit thou to faithful men, who shall be able to teach others also.

The Greek word for "commit" means "to deposit." You are to deposit what you have received "to faithful men," who, once they have received it, will "be able to teach others."

Notice that Paul did not tell Timothy to commit this responsibility to other preachers. No. God's plan for growth applies to every believer. Paul implies that Timothy should teach others, who should then teach yet others, who should teach even more people. We saw this strategy in Acts 2, where older believers taught the new believers, who turned around and taught other new believers.

Look at what Jesus told Peter in Luke 22:32.

> Luke 22:32
> But I have prayed for thee, that thy faith fail not:

and when thou art converted, strengthen thy brethren.

When you have gotten yourself right, make your brothers strong.

> Titus 2
> ¹But speak thou the things which become sound doctrine:
> ²That the aged men be sober, grave, temperate, sound in faith, in charity, in patience.
> ³The aged women likewise, that they be in behaviour as becometh holiness, not false accusers, not given to much wine, **teachers of good things**.

Paul is telling Titus to teach about issues of holiness, the *"things which become sound doctrine"* and they include men and women of God being *"teachers of good things."*

In 1 Timothy 3, Paul says that a man who wants to become a bishop must first exhibit the characteristics of a Christian man.

> 1 Timothy 3:2
> A bishop then must be blameless, the husband of one wife, vigilant, sober, of good behaviour, given to hospitality, **apt to teach**.

In 1 Thessalonians 2, Paul talks about the attitude he had in ministering to the people God brought across his path.

> 1 Thessalonians 2
> ⁷But we were gentle among you, even as a nurse

cherisheth her children:
⁸So being affectionately desirous of you, we were willing to have imparted unto you, not the gospel of God only, but also our own souls, because ye were dear unto us.

You should love people so much that you cannot wait to minister to them. You want to bless them. You want to encourage them. You want to give them sound doctrine. Paul said, "We were not just willing to give you the gospel, but also willing to give of our own souls because you are precious to us." Why? Because you are precious to God.

Below is a prophecy from Kenneth Copeland's *Believer's Voice of Victory* magazine which I would like to give to you.

> I need you, saith the Lord. I need every born-again child of God. I need you filled with the Spirit. I need you free from fear, doubt, unbelief, and all the bondages that you've known in the past. This is the grandest, greatest time. This is the time that I planned, saith the Lord.
>
> This is our time. I need you. There are more people coming into my kingdom right now than ever in the history of the relationship between heaven and earth. I need you. I need you to follow what I'm saying to you. I need you to be obedient to the spirit of grace. There are wonders and signs from heaven being prepared right now. There is coming a sudden shock wave in the kingdom of God that is going to flow out into the earth and there is going to be a sudden influx into the kingdom of God.

I need you. I need you ready. I need you prayed up and strong. I need you ready because there is going to be a flood of little brand-new born-again children coming into the kingdom of God. I need you to be a mother to them. I need you to be a father to them. I need you to be a big brother to them. I need you to be a big sister to them. I need you to help lead and guide and nurture them right on into this great tsunami of love and the power of God.[1]

So listen and be ready. Make adjustments in your life and in your lifestyle. Prepare, commit, and consecrate yourself. Reach out for a higher level in Me, saith the Lord. I need you and I need you strong, and My power is available to you as never before in the history of the human race. So rejoice, rejoice, rejoice, for the spirit of strength is among you.

Make a commitment to God today that you will become a teacher, a leader. You will serve. You will fulfill God's purpose for your life.

Chapter 4

Be Like Jesus and Get Your Twelve

The pastor alone cannot execute God's plan for church growth. God's plan is realized only when believers step up to their places of leadership. The Old Testament relates several instances where Moses could not get the job done alone. He needed the help of other people to win the battle and carry the weight of leadership.

One time (as recorded in Exodus 17), the nation of Israel was fighting a battle and Moses had the rod of God in his hand, which represented the anointing. As long as Moses kept his arm up, the Israelites would win, but whenever his arm came down, they would lose.

If the Israelites were winning, they were killing the enemy. If they were losing, they were dying. Aaron and Hur realized how tired Moses was and helped him hold up his arm until the battle was over and the Israelites had won.

Make no mistake: your willingness to be a leader is a matter of life and death; it is the difference between people's eternal salvation or their eternal damnation.

When believers in the church allow God to grow them up spiritually so that they become mature, when then they step out and teach and lead a Touch Group, when they consolidate new believers and help them grow up spiritually, they are helping the pastor and the ministerial staff keep up their arms. They are helping the people of God win. They are helping the kingdom of God increase throughout the earth.

In another instance, recorded in Numbers 11, the weight of being responsible for all the people became too much for Moses to bear. Moses said, "Look, God, if you are going to give me the responsibility of all these people, just kill me."

God said, "I want you to pick out seventy individuals, and I'll place your anointing upon those men. They will help you govern and be a blessing to the people." Moses was blessed, and the nation of Israel was blessed even more.

In yet another instance, recorded in Exodus 18, Moses was judging every matter of all the people every day. There were two to three million people in the nation of Israel at that time, and Moses' father-in-law, Jethro, said, "If you keep doing this you are going to wear yourself out and the people's needs will not be met, because you cannot see everybody. You need to appoint rulers of thousands, rulers of hundreds, rulers of fifties, and rulers of tens, and let them handle matters."

Growth Requires Team Effort

The church can embody the superstar mentality just as much as the world does. Some people think the pastor is supposed to do everything. They sit down and watch the superstar. However, one man, no matter who he is, cannot do it all.

If the players on a basketball team got the ball only into the hands of the superstar, they will not have a winning season, because one man cannot accomplish what a team can. A basketball team that works together, even if they have superstars on the team, keeps winning, because they realize that the team can do more than one person can do.

That is the revelation we have to get in the body of Christ. One pastor cannot do the job of reaching a whole city; nor can ten or twelve ministerial individuals. To win a city for God, every individual who comes through the church doors must allow God to grow him or her spiritually. Every individual must step up and become a teacher, a leader, in the body of Christ.

The Example of Jesus

Let's see specifically what we should be doing by looking at the greatest example there has ever been. Jesus Himself ministered for about two years without the help of other individuals. He had followers, but He did all the preaching, teaching, healing, casting out demons, and raising the dead. But God's plan was not that Jesus alone go forth and do these things forever. God's plan involved every believer rising up to become a teacher and leader.

> Matthew 9:35
> And Jesus went about all the cities and villages, teaching in their synagogues, and preaching the gospel of the kingdom, and healing every sickness and every disease among the people.

If there ever were a superstar, Jesus was one, but even He could not get the job done by Himself. He went about all the cities and all the villages. He was thorough. He was trying to reach everybody. The last two words in verse 35—"the people"—are the keys to motivation. Jesus had the people on His mind. They should be on our minds also.

Jesus was not just focused on the people he had already saved. He was focused on all of the lost. He did all of His traveling, all of His ministering, and all of His laying hands on people because He was thinking about them. His heart was moved with compassion for the lost.

In Matthew 9:35, Jesus was teaching, preaching, and healing in all the cities and villages He could get to. You might read this verse and think it should have ended by saying, "They lived happily ever after." Despite the fact that Jesus spent so much time and expended so much energy in trying to reach the lost—he ministered extensively for three and a half years—He was still living in a flesh-and-blood body. He could only do so much. His body got tired, just like ours do.

> Matthew 9:36
> But when he saw the multitudes, he was moved with compassion on them, because they fainted, and were scattered abroad, as sheep having no shepherd.

When Jesus saw the multitudes—lost individuals who hadn't received Him, people who were not walking in abundant life, prospering like God wanted them to and partnering with God in reaching the world—He was *"moved."* The Greek word for "moved" means "stirred emotionally."

All of us have been moved emotionally at one time or another, whether by watching a movie or football game or by watching our children. Jesus was not moved with sadness or anger; He was moved with compassion. The Amplified Bible says it this way:

> Matthew 9:36
> When He saw the throngs, He was moved with pity and sympathy for them, because they were

bewildered (harassed and distressed and dejected and helpless), like sheep without a shepherd.

A number of years ago I went overseas with several ministers. One of the places we visited was the city of Manila in the Philippines. I remember being in a van on the way to the hotel, in the middle of heavy traffic, with people on all sides, when I saw a little boy under a bridge, barely clothed, with a can in his hand. I was so moved with sympathy and pity that I wanted to stop the van, get that little boy, and bring him home with me.

When I walk and drive around the city where I pastor, I see many lost people who need Jesus in their lives. They are miserable, suffering, confused, and deceived. The harvest is ripe for the picking (John 4).

Jesus was moved with compassion over and over. He knew the people were lost and needy, like sheep that had been in a field for a long time without a shepherd. They were hungry and thirsty; they were confused and deceived, easily targeted by predators. Although He was the answer to having abundant life, He could not physically minister to all of them.

Look what Peter says about Jesus in Acts 10.

> Acts 10:38
> God anointed Jesus of Nazareth with the Holy Ghost and with power: who went about doing good, and healing all that were oppressed of the devil; for God was with him.

Satan is in the business of oppressing people. Jesus was moved by compassion because the people were oppressed. Satan was having his way in their life—stealing, killing, and destroying.

Most of the times when Jesus saw the multitudes, they were gathered in one spot. The fact that these multitudes were "scattered abroad" did not refer to their physical state; it referred to the fact that they had no direction, no guide, and no protection. They were not walking in the fullness of what God had for them.

> Matthew 9:37
> Then saith he unto his disciples, The harvest truly is plenteous, but the labourers are few.

In this verse, Jesus called the multitude *"the harvest."* Now He did not say *"the seed;"* He said *"the harvest"* because the harvest was ready for the picking. The people were ready to receive Jesus. They were ready to be disciples.

The fact that the harvest is plenteous means that there are still multitudes out there without Jesus. Jesus' problem, however, is not only that there are multitudes of people in a terrible spiritual state, but also that there are few laborers. Jesus can cover only so many. He is only one laborer.

Discipling the Twelve

> Matthew 10
> ¹And when he had called unto him his twelve disciples, he gave them power against unclean spirits, to cast them out, and to heal all manner of sickness and all manner of disease.
> ⁵These twelve Jesus sent forth, and commanded them, saying, Go not into the way of the Gentiles, and into any city of the Samaritans enter ye not.

Jesus equipped and sent forth twelve individuals to do what He was doing. He realized the principle that a group can do more together than one man working alone. In another passage, Jesus appointed seventy men to go out.

What did Jesus do next?

> Matthew 11:1
> And it came to pass, when Jesus had made an end of commanding his twelve disciples, he departed thence to teach and to preach in their cities.

Jesus did not just send out the twelve; He went back out Himself to build God's kingdom. Some people want to send others, but do not want to do anything themselves. Jesus commissioned and equipped the disciples and went out Himself because He loved the people and wanted more people to be blessed. His heart motivated him.

His heart continues to be moved with compassion. This is why He wants to raise you up as a teacher and a leader—so you can go forth and reach people with the gospel of Jesus Christ.

The Master Key to Success

What is the key to being a successful believer, teacher, and leader?

> Luke 6:12
> And it came to pass in those days, that he went out into a mountain to pray, and continued all night in prayer to God.

Every success is a prayer success. That is true in Touch Groups as well. In fact, being a leader will force you to grow in your prayer life. I had a prayer life when I started my ministry, but I prayed even more when I had to preach because I refused to get up in front of people without the anointing.

Being a leader, being responsible to people who are looking to you for help, will get you in the Word. It will get you on your knees. It will get you paying more attention to what goes on in church.

One reason some people do not grow much is that they can only grow so much when they're sitting in a pew. Playing only in practice will get you only so far, whether you are a basketball player or a Christian. Just as a basketball player has to step on the court in a game to realize his full potential, you have to get in the game as a believer to realize your potential.

The more you preach, the better you will get. The more you witness to God's grace and power, the better you will get.

Why did Jesus pray all night on the mountain?

> Matthew 6:13
> And when it was day, he called unto him his disciples: and of them he chose twelve, whom also he named apostles.

Notice this verse does not say that He called His twelve disciples. By this time Jesus had a multitude of followers. When He came down from the mountain, His followers were hanging out. He said, "Hey, come here!" and then chose twelve of them.

Those twelve were there with the rest of the followers. They heard all the teachings and saw all the miracles Jesus did. Yet that was not enough to prepare them to be like Jesus and to do

His works. Jesus, led by the Holy Ghost, selected these twelve men (see John 17).

Why Twelve?

The number seven is the number of completeness and perfection, but it is found only 60 times in Scripture. The number twelve is found 165 times. Why did Jesus select twelve men?

> Joshua 4
> ¹And it came to pass, when all the people were clean passed over Jordan, that the Lord spake unto Joshua, saying,
> ²Take you twelve men out of the people, out of every tribe a man,
> ³And command ye them, saying, Take you hence out of the midst of Jordan, out of the place where the priests' feet stood firm, twelve stones, and ye shall carry them over with you, and leave them in the lodging place, where ye shall lodge this night.
> ⁴Then Joshua called the twelve men, whom he had prepared of the children of Israel, out of every tribe a man.

God's promise to Abraham did not fully come to pass until there were twelve men, one from every tribe. The number twelve is the number of government in Scripture.

> 1 Kings 4:7
> And Solomon had twelve officers over all Israel, which provided victuals for the king and his household: each man his month in a year made provision.

Solomon's kingdom, a type of heaven—God's best—was run by twelve men.

> Matthew 19:28
> And Jesus said unto them, Verily I say unto you, That ye which have followed me, in the regeneration when the Son of man shall sit in the throne of his glory, ye also shall sit upon twelve thrones, judging the twelve tribes of Israel.

Jesus, speaking to his twelve disciples, told them that they would sit upon twelve thrones, judging the twelve tribes. Notice how the number twelve plays an integral role in the New Jerusalem.

> Revelation 21:12
> And had a wall great and high, and had twelve gates, and at the gates twelve angels, and names written thereon, which are the names of the twelve tribes of the children of Israel.

The Mission of the Twelve
What did Jesus have planned for these twelve disciples that was different from what He had planned for His other followers?

> Mark 1
> [16]Now as he walked by the sea of Galilee, he saw Simon and Andrew his brother casting a net into the sea: for they were fishers.
> [17]And Jesus said unto them, Come ye after me, and I will make you to become fishers of men.

Mark 3:14
And he ordained twelve, that they should be with him, and that he might send them forth to preach.

Ephesians 2
[19]Now therefore ye are no more strangers and foreigners, but fellowcitizens with the saints, and of the household of God;
[20]And are built upon the foundation of the apostles and prophets, Jesus Christ himself being the chief corner stone;
[21]In whom all the building fitly framed together groweth unto an holy temple in the Lord:
[22]In whom ye also are builded together for an habitation of God through the Spirit.

The early church was built on twelve men. Judas, one of the original disciples, betrayed Jesus, but in Acts 1 we read that the remaining eleven disciples chose another person to make twelve again. In the early chapters of Acts, the twelve were teaching, preaching, and healing.

When God called the twelve disciples, His plan was to make them fishers of men, like Jesus. His plan was to send them forth to preach, like Jesus. His plan was to make them the foundation of the church, like Jesus was.

In *The Ladder to Success* by Cesar Castellanos, the man to whom God revealed the principle of the twelve and pastor of a 500,000 member church in Bogota, Colombia, we read:

> Jesus won twelve men in whom he reproduced his character, and who became his representatives to the whole world. He transmitted his vision to the

twelve so that they could in turn transmit it to twelve others. In this way he achieved multiplication.[1]

Jesus preached to the multitudes, but He consolidated twelve, He discipled twelve, and He sent twelve. He gave special training to the twelve. There are many times in Scripture when we read about Jesus sitting down with the twelve, teaching them about the greatest in the kingdom, teaching them about the last days—teaching them about many things.

Why did Jesus choose twelve? Pastor Casellanos, commenting upon Matthew 9, says:

> The Lord saw the people and had compassion on them. That is why he chose twelve men to meet their needs. He gave them authority, then sent them out to expel demons and heal every sickness. Jesus invested most of his ministry in forming these twelve disciples. He had a very specific goal, which was to reproduce his character in the lives of these twelve men.[2]

Jesus worked at forming these twelve leaders; He took time to personally disciple the twelve. Notice how Jesus took responsibility for the twelve in John 17:12.

> John 17:12
> While I was with them in the world, I kept them in thy name: those that thou gavest me I have kept, and none of them is lost, but the son of perdition; that the scripture might be fulfilled.

Jesus goes on to say, "Father, I pray that you keep them, as I kept Myself holy for them."

> John 17:18
> As thou hast sent me into the world, even so have I also sent them into the world.

As a Christian, you are called, and you are sent.

The Principle of Twelve

In 1991, Pastor Castellanos visited the world's largest church in Seoul, South Korea, pastored by Dr. David Cho. When he discovered that Dr. Cho's church had grown through cell groups, Pastor Castellanos incorporated that system in his church, with mild success. After seven years he had only seventy groups. Only about 30 percent of the church was involved in cell groups. He went to God in prayer and asked, "How do we get to the next level?"

God asked him, "How many people did you see Jesus disciple?"

"Twelve," Pastor Castellanos responded.

"So, do you think you should be winning more than twelve or less than twelve?"[3]

God then began to reveal to him that Jesus did not train the multitudes. He only trained the twelve.

God then said, "If you train twelve people and you manage to reproduce in them the character of Christ which is in you, and if every one of them does the same with another twelve people, and if these in turn do the same with another twelve, transmitting the same vision to others, you and your church will experience unprecedented growth."[4]

Pastor Castellanos identified twelve leaders and began to train and disciple them, to pour his life into his leaders. From that point, his church experienced exponential growth, going from 70 groups in 1991 to 1,200 groups three years later. In the next two years, they grew to 4,000 groups. In 1996, cell groups grew from 4,000 to 10,500. Three years later in 1999, the church had 20,000 groups. Pastor Castellanos' church has grown so much that they count only cell groups now, not number of members!

This is the principle of twelve. If every person trained and discipled twelve people, who in turn discipled twelve people (at Faith Christian Center, this discipleship system has been termed J-12), we would realize exponential growth in the body of Christ. But in order to train twelve people, to reproduce in them the character of Christ, the character of Christ must be in you. That is why you have to grow up yourself, to allow someone to train or disciple you, to be mature. That is why you must be involved in a Touch Group and attend J-12 meetings.

This is how Jesus operated. He called His twelve one by one. In Luke 5, Jesus had been teaching people out of Peter's boat, and when he finished preaching, he told Peter: *"Launch out into the deep, and let down your nets for a draught" (Luke 5:4)*. Peter obeyed Jesus, and received a miracle of fishes. Jesus told Peter that from that point on he would be a fisher of men. Jesus then went on to win Philip, Andrew, and the rest of His twelve.

Being a Fruit-Bearer

You do not need to go out and find twelve disciples tomorrow. Jesus brought forth much fruit, but He called individuals one by one, or sometimes two at a time. Your goal is also to bring forth fruit—people you can develop into mature leaders for Christ.

Notice that Jesus did not call men who were already established in the faith, but He did pray that they would be faithful. Notice Jesus' words to Peter:

> Luke 22
> [31]And the Lord said, Simon, Simon, behold, Satan hath desired to have you, that he may sift you as wheat:
> [32]But I have prayed for thee, that thy faith fail not: and when thou art converted, strengthen thy brethren.

Many of us are here today because of Jesus' prayers. Likewise, because of your prayers, many believers who might have given up will be here tomorrow.

Believer, you are to be like Jesus. You are to win your twelve and get them established in the faith. Jesus did not call you out just so you could be blessed. If you do not have time to train and disciple leaders, you do not have time to be blessed. You are not pleasing to God. Being a Christian is not just going to church on Sunday and turning to God when you are in trouble; being a Christian is about winning the lost and making disciples. Being a Christian is about being a fisher of men, preaching the gospel and raising up people. Being a Christian is about building the kingdom.

Now the principle of small groups has been around the church for a long time, and we have been doing Touch Groups from the beginning in the church I pastor. While Dr. Cho has popularized the principle of cell groups, the principle of going from house to house is throughout the New Testament—we operate according to the Book.

I first heard about the principle of twelve in a church in Tulsa that was the second or third largest cell group church in the country. I and some other pastors discussed the doctrinal reasons why we did not like this system, but a couple of years later when asked if I had ever incorporated this system into my church, I received a check from the Spirit when I said, "No." I went back and studied the Word and found out that I had been wrong. The principle of twelve is found throughout Scripture. I then read Pastor Castellanos' book, and the Spirit of God dealt with me and said, "This is the vision I have for your church. These are the principles I want you to follow." That was the beginning of our Path to Leadership program.

Now, the Principle of Twelve may not be the system or the vision for every church, but every church should be meeting from house to house. The largest churches in this country all operate according to the system of cell groups.

> Proverbs 11:30
> The fruit of the righteous is a tree of life; and he that winneth souls is wise.

Notice that Scripture does not say, "He that winneth one soul is wise." It says, "He that winneth souls [many people] is wise." In order to be like Jesus and get your twelve, you are going to need to have your own Touch Group. When you get your twelve, help them get their twelve, send them out to start their own groups. Then instead of being a leader of twelve, you will be a leader of 144. The body of Christ grows when believers decide to be like Jesus and bring forth fruit.

One of the members of Pastor Castellanos' church in Bogota was a youth who worked as a custodian. She had 80 cell groups under her. This is how you get 100,000 members in a church:

believers have to decide to be like Jesus and go and bring forth fruit!

> Daniel 12:3
> And they that be wise shall shine as the brightness of the firmament; and they that turn many to righteousness as the stars for ever and ever.

God's will is that you turn many to righteousness and that you make many disciples.

> 1 John 2:6
> He that saith he abideth in him ought himself also so to walk, even as he walked.

Walk like Jesus walked. Heal like Jesus healed. Teach like Jesus taught. Disciple like Jesus discipled. Jesus won twelve, He consolidated twelve, and He discipled twelve. The Gospels are full of stories of Jesus sitting with the twelve and teaching them many things about the Kingdom.

Be like Jesus. Only then will God's strategy for building the church be a reality.

Salvation Prayer

If you do not know Jesus as your Lord and Savior, simply pray the following prayer in faith and Jesus will be your Lord!

Heavenly Father, I come to you in the name of Jesus. Your Word says, 'Whosoever shall call on the name of the Lord shall be saved' and 'If thou shalt confess with thy mouth the Lord Jesus, and shalt believe in thine heart that God hath raised him from the dead, thou shalt be saved (Acts 2:21, Romans 10:9).' You said salvation would be the result of Your Holy Spirit giving me new birth by coming to live in me (John 3:5-6, 14-16, Romans 8:9-11) and that if I would ask, You would fill me with Your Spirit and give me the ability to speak with other tongues (Luke 11:13, Acts 2:4).

I take You at Your Word. I confess that Jesus is Lord. And I believe in my heart that You raised Him from the dead. Thank You for coming into my heart, for giving me Your Holy Spirit as You have promised, and for being Lord over my life.

If you have just prayed this prayer, please let us know of your decision by contacting us at:

Faith Christian Center
3059 S. Cobb Drive
Smyrna, GA 30080
www.fccga.com

APPENDIX

Touch Group Testimonies
Part I

The following testimonies were delivered at Faith Christian Center in Smyrna, Georgia, during Pastor Butler's sermon series on "God's Plan for the Church."

My husband was in the US Army when we joined Faith Christian Center in January 2002. He was deployed in March of that year, and I thought, *What am I going to do with two small children and a husband away in the war?* I joined Touch Group, and it was such a blessing. Touch Group members were my babysitters, helping me with the children and calling me every week.

When I e-mailed my husband about all the support they were giving me, he replied, "Oh, I'm missing out! I can't wait to get back. Who are these people?" When he got back they loved on him, and we were full of support and comfort.

Through participating in Touch Group and going to different members' homes, I have met many people. We've prayed for one another and loved one another. We are compassionate toward one another. Three family members received Christ and joined satellite churches through the prayers of Touch Group members, so we've been really blessed.

We bought a home in January of 2005; shortly after that, my husband was deployed again for three months. This time I said to myself, *Okay, I can do this.* My Touch Group family will be here.

My husband and I were believing God to provide livingroom furniture, and it wasn't long before our Touch Group leader called. She said, "There is someone who has furniture and has rarely used it, and he wants to give that to you." Once again, God provided for us through Touch Group.

I want to encourage you to go to a Touch Group, because in church you don't have the fellowship and family atmosphere you have in Touch Group. Our Touch Group members even see one another outside of Touch Group, and it is been a wonderful blessing.

– P. Birdsong

I didn't want to have anything to do with Touch Group when I came to this church. I really wasn't inclined to join the church because I thought it was too big—I'm from the South, and I'm used to the little home church. I thought, *I'll never get to know anybody in this church.*

Now, coming to church is fine, but you have to take your commitment beyond the four walls of the church. Touch Group is a vehicle that the Lord will use to help you come into contact with other people. It will help you be delivered; it will help you be set free from many things. That's what it did for my wife and me.

Some people say, "The church is too large. I don't get a chance to meet Pastor Butler and know his heart." That may be the case, but participating in a Touch Group allows you to see and understand the pastor's heart. Attending Touch Group is not about you and it is not about me; it is about being hooked up with the vision. I want to encourage you to get hooked up with this vision and get hooked up with the ministry. In turn, you will get hooked up with the heart of the pastor.

– C. Birdsong

I remember coming to the church and knowing no one. I got saved here in 2000, and as soon as I got saved I made the comment, "Man, you know what? I have tried everything in the world and it didn't work, so I might as well try this." I wanted to try this; it was just so awesome. But I still didn't know a single person. I came to church, got the Word, went home, and got excited.

I started hearing about Touch Groups, and God put in my heart that I needed to be a part of one. I got directions to four different groups, and for three weeks straight I got lost every time I tried to go.

Then one week I said, "I'm going to go to Touch Group no matter what." I took six different directions and I left extra early. I finally made it to a Touch Group. It was fun, food, and fellowship, but it was also much more than that.

Faith Christian Center is a huge church, but at the same time, it is a small church. When you go to Touch Group you bond with people of like faith and you develop friendships even closer than family, and that causes you to be more effective. If you are going through something you can say, "Hey, pray for me," and be frank about it, and you will be delivered. But if all you do is just come to church, you are missing out on 90 percent of what God has for you.

I was in school full time and worked full time, and I thought, *I don't have the time to go to Touch Group.* The next thought, however, was, *I have still got to go.* It is so fulfilling to not only be blessed myself but also to see people around me get really blessed, people who really need it.

Whether you are married or not, you need to be in a Touch Group because you cannot be a Christian by yourself. By coming to Touch Group and being ministered to and ministering to other people, you will see yourself being set free in areas that you never even knew you had issues with. You need Touch Group—that's the bottom line.

– G. DeCosta

Part II

The following testimonies were submitted anonymously by Touch Group Leaders. While reading them, look for the ways that God is using Touch Groups to provide fellowship, accountability, encouragement, understanding of the Word, and discipling opportunities.

A first time-visitor to my Touch Group reported that she had to move and didn't know how she would do this or where she would go. She had to be out of her place by Tuesday morning, and it was already Monday evening. Upon hearing this, I called a few Women of Virtue and my husband called three Men of Valor, saying, "One of my wife's

Touch Group attendees needs to move now, and I need your help."

One of the Women of Virtue gave a hundred dollars towards moving expenses, and others came to help, bringing boxes and plenty of plastic tubs with lids. I went to three different truck rental places to find a truck, but by the time I got to the third place, the office had already been closed almost half an hour. The Spirit said, "Go back and knock on the window." When I did, the manager unlocked the door and asked, "How may I help you?"

He gave me a big truck for no charge and no contract, telling me only to have the truck back in the morning. He then gave me a number to call if anything happened, but I said, "Nothing will happen! I have angels working with me!" Upon hearing my declaration, he asked me what church I attended!

My husband called to tell me that he had a house full of people ready to help, and I replied, "Keep praying!" and told him where to meet me.

When I pulled up with the U-Haul, the look on the faces in the group was priceless, because they thought they were going to be moving this woman's furniture and belongings in a pick-up truck owned by one of the Men of Valor. The young lady whom we were helping was amazed and said "Our church seem big, but it is not big at all!"

We moved her out of a two-bedroom apartment full of furniture in fifty minutes. While still in her parking lot, we put her in the middle of the group with the Women of Virtue around her and the Men of Valor around us, and closed with prayer.

My hat goes off to the Men of Valor. While we were moving this young woman, men were still calling with offers to help. The whole experience added a new meaning to "Teaching the Word, Doing the Work, and Touching the World!"

❦

The lesson in our last Touch Group meeting was very interesting and special. The participation was anointed. Even participants who usually don't have much to say had many examples of how to be like Jesus. This lesson encouraged us to look to the hills from which comes our help.

❦

Covenant Partners Touch Group was high and anointed. We opened in prayer. The facilitation was wonderful and the responses to the questions were great. All the couples interacted and effectively communicated during the ice-breaker question. The children were taught the Word and they all participated in reciting a Bible verse. We really had an awesome time and give thanks and praise to our heavenly Father for a wonderful time of fun, food, and fellowship.

❦

At the last Touch Group meeting, an attendee asked for prayer for a cough that had developed for no known reason. We prayed about it before ending the meeting. He stated that by the next morning the cough was completely gone!

※

Our touch group prayed for one member to get a car, and by the next meeting she had a new car that she drove to the meeting! Another attendee received news that a pending accident case she was involved in three years ago was finally being settled this week and she would be receiving a substantial sum of money.

※

Cynita was able to minister salvation to someone on her return trip from Detroit.

※

An attendee's great-grandmother, who is ninety-two years old, had a stroke and then a heart attack. The attendee was told she had died, only to get a phone call a few hours later telling her that her great-grandmother was not dead but in stable condition and had returned home.

※

One day this summer, there was a major accident on I-285 that shut down traffic going north for most of the day. The morning of the accident, I was urged in my spirit to immediately get up and get going. I didn't even brush up and wash my face. When I was driving to work, I began to pass a semi-truck. While I passed the truck, by mere seconds at the least, the truck ran across the highway toward the median and flipped over. If I had been one or two seconds slower, the truck would have wiped me out completely. When the truck turned over it blocked all the lanes. Praise God, those two seconds were the difference between my life and my getting ahead of the truck. I wasn't even late for work.

After LaRunda and another attendee prayed together for her to have more boldness and step out in faith to interview for a higher position on her job, she did and got the job the same day.

A member of our Touch Group got a brand-new car. Another member received a large check that she was not expecting.

One of the prayer requests made during prayer by an attendee was that a friend of hers would rededicate his life to Christ since he was going through some personal challenges. The next Sunday during altar call, he went down and rededicated his life to Christ. He now wants to become a member of Faith Christian Center.

An attendee offered a ride home to a young lady because it was raining. In transit, she told her about Touch Group and where she was going. The young lady was having some challenges and said that she would love to come for prayer. We prayed for her in the meeting and believe that there was deliverance and peace from the challenges she was having. Thank God for divine interventions.

One attendee had been exhausted, pressing through with work, getting her master's degree, and dealing with her son's carnal lifestyle. She prayed for God's strength and presence. That evening, her son called her and told her that his college teacher held up his work assignment as an example of excellence. That same evening, the attendee attended her class and her professor did the same thing—held up a paper she had worked on for a long time and cited it as an example of excellence. When she got home, she and her son had a Holy Ghost praise party as they shared success brought by God. This outcome was encouraging and an indication of God's presence and favor in their lives.

Since the last meeting, both the Touch Group leader and her daughter received new cars after prayer about the matter. Praise the Lord!

We are having great discussions in our Touch Group and are experiencing an increase of members. Every prayer request they have and we pray for is answered. Some of the new visitors have come back just to tell us what God did for them. Glory to God!

❧

We had "hot seat" prayer for two attendees with challenges in their bodies. One attendee experienced immediate healing in her back. She was able to bend and touch her toes without pain, something she could not do upon arrival. Hallelujah!

❧

One attendee has been praying and believing God to work in the field of marketing. She was asked to put together a marketing project, was successful with that project, and received a promotion and a pay increase. Another attendee confessed that she and her boyfriend were convicted in Sunday's service about living together and not being married. She reported that the next week she and her boyfriend were going to the justice of the peace to get married. Praise God!

❧

When the Touch Group leader asked for prayer requests, two youths asked for prayer to get after-school jobs. To their surprise, another attendee hired both of them on the spot! One attendee asked for prayer to receive help in taking care of her very active baby. Immediately, another attendee volunteered to babysit so she could get some rest one day a week.

❧

A Touch Group leader received unexpected income after sowing a seed in the lives of two homeless women with children. Hallelujah!

❧

The Touch Group meeting yesterday was wonderful and a blessing to all who attended. All attendees participated in the sharing question and the facilitation. The sharing question was a great icebreaker, and during facilitation we had people who would normally say very little interact with one another quite a bit more. More husbands seemed to be open and actually had a lot to say. We closed with prayer requests and prayer. Then we had a little surprise for our newest newlywed attendee, Kim. She and her husband were blessed with a cake, cards, and nice gifts. She was very excited! It was a blessed evening of fun, food, and fellowship. We give our heavenly Father all the glory, honor, and praise for it.

❧

We prayed in our Touch Group meeting for Shannon and Dabreen to get jobs, and both reported new jobs were secured by the next meeting.

❧

Appendix: Touch Group Testimonies

We prayed for one attendee to receive her long-awaited accident check, and she reported that the check arrived the day of the Touch Group meeting.

෴

Two attendees asked for prayer for employment at the last meeting, and both received jobs.

෴

One attendee received a promotion and received a $12,000 raise. The Touch Group prayed for another attendee's cousin, who was diagnosed with cancer. At her next visit, the doctors said she did not have cancer but a less severe condition. She also was laid off from her job when she was diagnosed. She was offered her job back and received a raise. A third attendee received a $25,000 raise and has had the opportunity to minister the Word to coworkers. Glory to God!

෴

Wanda was believing God to provide the means for her to attend a work-related conference. The Holy Spirit moved upon the heart of another coworker, who gave her a financial blessing!

෴

Sharon received an unexpected financial blessing in her workplace. Because of God's favor, her contract was renewed and subsequently she was given a pay raise and additional vacation time. To God be the glory!

Two new Christians, Donald and Tawyna, came to Touch Group, and we asked the husband to do the closing prayer of blessing. Afterward we told him he did an awesome prayer. Everyone shared about being open and honest with their spouses. Our Touch Group leader received an exceptional rating for his yearly evaluation as well as a 7 percent raise and 6 percent bonus. Another couple bought an investment property that we had previously prayed about. We did the "hot seat" prayer for that couple as well the wife of the visiting couple.

One member gave a testimony that she and her husband had been in the process of buying a house and they were told they issues concerning their credit. She was praying and God told her to sow a seed of $29. She did, and the same day she was called and told that she was approved for her home.

One attendee got a brand-new car, another got a new job, and another was blessed with someone paying off her credit card. Yet another signed papers to establish his own company. God also blessed our leader exceedingly abundantly above anything he could have imagined. Our Touch Group leader was hired as a division-one assistant men's basketball coach without the head coach even looking at his resume. There were more than 250 applicants. God told him to call the head coach (he didn't even know he was hiring), and he interviewed him that day and hired him the next day. The job is exactly what he had been believing God for, and it came with a $10,000 raise from his current job.

One attendee received healing at the meeting. Another was offered a bigger home for less money. Another attendee was able to sign a contract for a rental property for a great price. Another attendee registered for college in one day when it usually takes a week. An attendee was blessed with an apartment in a good neighborhood (close to school and church) at a below-market price. Another attendee, who is unemployed, received unexpected income.

Our Touch Group had an awesome testimony from a young lady who had been disowned by her family and found her way to us through the persistent encouragement of another attendee.

A member of our group had been in need of consistent transportation since the beginning of the year, and the Lord blessed him with a car for only $200.

One attendee's husband attended Thursday-night service for the first time, one received a raise five times this year, one received debt cancellation, one conceived a child after eighteen years of marriage, and one received a monetary special-act award in a temporary position from her manager.

One of our members, Sheila, was blessed with a car paid in full.

During our Touch Group meeting tonight, a participant was experiencing a severe headache. We stopped our lesson and laid hands on her, and the headache subsided. Another participant had been without her car for over a month. At the last Touch Group meeting we prayed about her car being completed and returned to her. She now has her car back and received a discount from the mechanic for the repair cost.

One attendee said that because of the prayers of Touch Group her son does not have to go back to Iraq; his assignment has been changed to stay in the States and he's up for rank. Glory to God! God is so good!

Trashon and another Touch Group member were praying by his car after meeting, and a first-time visitor, Lois, walked by who was in need of prayer. She began to cry uncontrollably, but after we prayed with her she smiled and we could see that God had lifted the burden from her. We told her about Faith Christian Center, Pastor Butler, and Touch Group, and the next week she came to our Touch Group meeting and said it was a blessing. She also said that she would be coming to visit Faith Christian Center.

Two people received promotions on their jobs, and one person's father-in-law was healed of cancer through prayer at Touch Group before he was admitted to the hospital.

An attendee received a job promotion.

Our Touch Group leader was reminded by a previous attendee that a word had gone forth in a previous meeting by the Spirit of the Lord, prophesying that a major change was coming on the job where the leader would be elevated to a position that is greater than what he had even imagined. The persecution he was enduring at the hands of his superiors would cease. It was also prophesied that his new position would place his enemy as a footstool under his feet. God would be glorified in this elevation because it would be supernatural. This leader stated he is now over his persecutors because the company created a position and placed him in it at the corporate headquarter level, much to the amazement of everyone. Glory to God! He is faithful to perform His word.

᪣

Nina has a new job, and Nina and Amber received healings at the meeting.

᪣

We had a small youth Touch Group but the anointing was there. The young men had an opportunity to share their dreams and we were able to pray for God's purpose to be revealed to them. They've even made decisions to begin serving in Glorify God auxiliaries.

᪣

While we discussed the importance of discovering our purpose and not letting anyone distract us from it, we learned that many blessings are tied to our purpose, and many lives are negatively affected when we do not flow with our purpose.

᪣

We prayed for those who desired jobs, praying that their jobs would not take them away from God, their family, or school. The next day, an attendee was hired and her hours will not interfere with her serving, family, or school work.

᪣

NOTES

Introduction
1. *Consolidation* is "the care and attention we should give every new believer in order to reproduce in him the character of Christ with the aim that he fulfill the purpose of God for his life, which is to bear fruit that endures." Consolidation is the very foundation for discipling and the first part of discipleship.

Chapter 3
1. Kenneth Copeland, "I Need You", *Kenneth Copeland Ministries,* March 18, 2005, *http://www.kcm.org/studycenter/ prophecies/20050318bransonvc.php.*

Chapter 4
1. Cesar Castellanos, *The Ladder to Success.* (Columbia, South America: Editorial Vilit & Co. Ltd., 2001), 46.
2. Ibid., 164.
3. Ibid., 25.
4. Ibid.

FAITH CHRISTIAN CENTER
PATH TO LEADERSHIP

STEPS TO BECOMING AN EFFECTIVE LEADER AT FAITH CHRISTIAN CENTER INCLUDE:

STEP 1
COMPLETE PRE-ENCOUNTER CLASSES

COURSE BOOK
God's Plan for the Church

STEP 2
ATTEND AN ENCOUNTER

COURSE BOOK
Winning the War Within

STEP 3
COMPLETE POST-ENCOUNTER CLASSES

COURSE BOOK
J-12: Be Like Jesus, Get Your 12

STEP 4
COMPLETE SCHOOL OF JESUS YEAR 1 CLASS I

COURSE BOOK
Becoming Like Jesus

STEP 5
ATTEND A LEADER'S ENCOUNTER

STEP 6
COMPLETE SCHOOL OF JESUS CLASS II
START A TOUCH GROUP

COURSE BOOK
The One Another Principle
A Friend to Sinners

STEP 7
COMPLETE SCHOOL OF JESUS CLASS III
(GRADUATION)

COURSE BOOK
Fervent in Spirit
Be Like Jesus

YOU ARE A *LEADER!*
NOW GO FORTH AND GET YOUR **12!**

About the Author

From an early age, Pastor Andre Butler was aware of an anointing and commissioning by God to spread the good news of Jesus Christ. An outstanding student, Pastor Butler received a full academic scholarship to the University of Michigan, but God instructed him to attend Rhema Bible Training Center in Oklahoma in preparation to answer God's call to ministry. Obediently, he graduated from Rhema Bible Training Center in 1996, where he was a member of the men's basketball team.

Shortly thereafter, Pastor Butler was privileged with the opportunity to serve as a minister at Word of Faith International Christian Center in Michigan. As a young minister, he founded a singles' ministry for young adults between the ages of eighteen and twenty-five, today known as Entheos. He also founded a college ministry that has expanded to more than eight campuses across the United States. Along with his father, Pastor Butler now co-pastors Word of Faith, currently located on a 110-acre campus with more than 22,000 members and 16 satellite churches.

In 2001, Pastor Butler was promoted to the senior pastor of Faith Christian Center, located in Smyrna, Georgia founded by Bishop Butler in 1993. In addition to pastoring Faith Christian Center, co-pastoring Word of Faith, and being a loving husband and father, Pastor Butler attended classes at Kennesaw State University and graduated with a bachelor's degree in management in 2004.

Faith Christian Center now has more than 3,000 members. In his ministry, Pastor Butler is called to emphasize God's desire to prosper His people in every area of life and the importance of studying and obeying the Word of God. The heart of his vision is to win, consolidate, disciple, and send out believers to win the world to Jesus. To help realize this vision, he founded the J-12 discipleship program based on small group home meetings called Touch Groups where leaders are encouraged to become a leader of twelve. He's also a strong advocate of the Path to Leadership program where members are trained extensively to become spiritually mature men and women of God who actively fulfill God's purpose and mission for their lives.

With the support of his anointed wife, Minister Tiffany N. Butler, and their two precious daughters, Alexis Nichol and Angela Marie, Pastor Butler ministers in churches and conferences throughout the United States and abroad.

FAITH CHRISTIAN CENTER

CATALOG

TEACHING THE WORD, DOING THE WORK, TOUCHING THE WORLD

INCREASE IN YOUR VICTORY

WINNING THE WAR WITHIN

If you are facing a problem that has defeated you time and time again - from fornication to low self-esteem - this book is for you. This book is designed to teach you how to defeat the only enemy that can stop you from being successful - YOU! Receive and apply this mind-renewing truth from the Word of God, then experience breakthroughs to the next level of Christian living and victory upon victory in your life!

INCREASE IN YOUR PURPOSE

GETTING TO YOUR PROMISED LAND

God has a Promised Land for you, and it represents His perfect will for your life. Getting there is one of the master keys to living the prosprous life that God wants you to have. In this book, you'll read how God has a purpose for your life, a ministry that only you can fulfill. When you follow God's plan for your life, you can then claim the full measure of all the blessings that He wants you to have - restoration, healing, and more!

INCREASE IN YOUR FAITH

REVEALED KNOWLEDGE: THE MISSING ELEMENT

It greatly pleases our heavenly Father when we receive His blessings. However, the lives of many believers seem to be characterized by a missing element, something stopping God's power from working in their lives. If you are one of these believers, the purpose of this book is to identify that missing element, to tell you how to get it, and to tell you how to use it. This book will help you receive all the blessings God wants you to have and enjoy heaven on earth in your life.

FOR MORE INFORMATION, PLEASE VISIT WWW.FCCGA.COM, CALL 770.433.8800 OR WRITE FAITH CHRISTIAN CENTER, 3059 S. COBB DRIVE, SMYRNA, GA 30080.

INCREASE IN YOUR SINGLENESS

GOD'S PLAN FOR THE SINGLE SAINT

As a single believer, have you ever wondered, 'Has God forgotten me?' or 'Does He even know where I am?' You don't have to feel hopeless because God has a definite plan and design for your life. His plan is to prepare and fulfill you as a Christian single so you can be happy and fullfilled as a Christian mate!

INCREASE IN YOUR MINISTRY

FOR PK'S ONLY: A BOOK FOR THE NEXT GENERATION
COAUTHORED WITH
MIN. MICHELLE BUTLER

Having grown up in a minister's home themselves, Keith and MiChelle Butler discuss openly such issues as meeting the unrealistic expectations of others; dealing with the "fish bowl-," "doorway-," and "low self-esteem-syndromes"; and exercising forgiveness when betrayed by someone you trusted. These young authors, now in the ministry themselves, offer proven solutions from the Word of God to these unique problems.

INCREASE IN YOUR FINANCES

THE RIGHT WAY TO GIVE

God wants to bless you! God wants you to be prosperous! However, in order to receive His blessings in your life, you must give in accordance with the instructions found in the Word of God. The Right Way to Give is a step-by-step guide showing you those steps found in God's Word. Your faith will be strengthened as you read examples found in Scripture that illustrate the right way to give. And as you follow these examples, you will find that God will bless you to be a blessing!

GAINING FINANCIAL FREEDOM

Are you working only to pay off your debts, living from paycheck to paycheck? Are you existing on a financial plateau, lacking nothing but unable to give to others? If so, this booklet is for you! God's will is that you be a financial dominator for the Kingdom of God. Although you can not serve God and money, you can serve God with your money.

GOD IS MAKING YOU RICH

Are you struggling to stay in faith concerning the financial harvest God has promised you? Do your circumstances seem to be getting bigger in your eyes while God's promises seem to get smaller? Is the enemy whispering in your ear that you will never walk in abundance? If any of these statements fit you then 'God is Making You Rich' is the book for you! In this book, Pastor Butler II uses the Word of God to build your faith for the financial harvest God has promised you.

WEALTH OF THE SINNER, HARVEST OF THE JUST

God's Word promises that when his children give He will deal with men to give unto them in a multiplied measure. Nowhere in the Word does it say that only other believers would be used to financially bless His children. In fact, an in depth study of Scripture reveals that many times The Wealth of the Sinner, and The Harvest of the Just are the same thing. This book by Pastor Butler II will reveal to you how to Receive the Wealth of the World to Reach the World for Jesus!

SEEDTIME & HARVEST

Have you been sowing SEED into the Kingdom of God for years without receiving the fullness of your HARVEST? God's will for your life is that you not just receive the 'Good Measure' promised in Luke 6:38 but the 'Running Over.' That you not receive just '30-fold' but '100-fold' returns. In this book, Pastor Butler II explores the principles to God's financial system and the Keys to Receiving the Fullness of the Harvest God has promised you. Read to be abundantly blessed and to use that blessing to spread the Gospel of the Kingdom of God!

FOR MORE INFORMATION, PLEASE VISIT WWW.FCCGA.COM, CALL 770.433.8800 OR WRITE FAITH CHRISTIAN CENTER, 3059 S. COBB DRIVE, SMYRNA, GA 30080.